PROVERBS
FOR BUSINESS

STEVE MARR

SPIRE

© 2001 by Steve Marr

Published by Fleming H. Revell
a division of Baker Publishing Group
P.O. Box 6287, Grand Rapids, MI 49516-6287
www.revellbooks.com

Spire edition published 2006
ISBN 10: 0-8007-8751-X
ISBN 978-0-8007-8751-6

Fourth printing, July 2007

Previously printed under the title *Business Proverbs*

Printed in the United States of America

To my wife, Mary, without whose love,
encouragement, and friendship *Proverbs for Business*
would not have been possible.

⚬〰〰⚬

Introduction

Being employed in today's workplace means spending
a majority of your waking hours on the job. *Proverbs for Business* was written to assist those working at all levels of an
organization, from owner, CEO, or manager to the newest
employee. Each page contains information based on a principle designed to apply to most work circumstances and is
intended to give you practical advice in a short format. You
may access expanded business proverbs topics or find
answers to commonly asked business questions at my
businessproverbs.com web site.

Early in my career I learned solid business ethics from
my dad and most business lessons on the street of hard
knocks. *Proverbs for Business* is designed to provide practical business application with the authority of the Scriptures. The Bible is still the best business book!

The signature Scripture for *Proverbs for Business* is Joshua 1:8. It is a reminder that the Holy Bible still provides the wisdom necessary for every aspect of our lives, including time we spend on our jobs. I have found that many business people are seeking ancient wisdom for today's competitive, success-driven workplace. In the Old Testament King Solomon, best known for building the grand temple in Jerusalem, became the wisest man in history. He was also "manager extraordinaire." While he completed vast projects and expanded the kingdom, he remained at peace with his neighbors. The queen of Sheba visited Solomon and learned that Scripture was the basis for his great wealth and accomplishment. She ultimately gave glory to the God of Israel for everything she observed.

Likewise, we need to read, understand, and adopt biblical business principles in our workplace environment today. Reading each page, digesting Scripture, and applying the *Proverbs for Business* principles will enhance your performance on the job. Your customers, employees, and managers will begin to experience increased business effectiveness. When others see your improvement, give glory to the Lord!

Have you considered the competition before starting a new business venture?

Scripture: What king, when he sets out to meet another king in battle, will not first sit down and take counsel whether he is strong enough with ten thousand men to encounter the one coming against him with twenty thousand? (Luke 14:31).

Today's Thought: The biblical principle of "counting the cost" applies to business situations as well as spiritual decisions. When launching a new venture or expanding a current business, it's wise to first evaluate existing competitors, as well as those who might join the battle later.

Here are some key questions to answer: Do I have enough capital to launch and sustain my business? Do I understand my product's niche in the market? Can I weather the competition? Can I deliver the necessary quality and level of service? Can I carry the selection my customers will demand?

Counting the cost before you begin can help to avoid an expensive mistake.

Each circumstance will be different, but every new venture requires a careful analysis of your own capabilities and the realities of the marketplace. Don't be caught short. Counting the cost before you begin can help to avoid an expensive mistake.

For by wise guidance you will wage war, and in abundance of counselors there is victory (Proverbs 24:6).

Do you take care of small problems before they become big ones?

Scripture: What woman, if she has ten silver coins and loses one coin, does not light a lamp and sweep the house and search carefully until she finds it? (Luke 15:8).

Today's Thought: A popular saying in today's business environment is "Don't sweat the small stuff." If we miss on a bid, we shrug it off; if we lose a customer . . . well, they were too much trouble anyway. Unfortunately, if we allow this attitude to fester, small losses turn into big problems, and our business will suffer.

When you adopt the principle of "taking care of the little things," success will soon follow.

A contrary principle to "don't sweat the small stuff" is "take care of the little things, and the big things will take care of themselves." When small losses are not acceptable—when we attend to things at the first sign of trouble and don't give up until the problem is solved—those small losses don't have a chance to grow.

Take action today. Call a customer you've lost and win him back. Look again to find that missing inventory. Call one more time to collect that past due bill. When you adopt the principle of "taking care of the little things," success will soon follow.

Deliver yourself like a gazelle from the hunter's hand, and like a bird from the hand of the fowler (Proverbs 6:5).

Do you faithfully give your customers a full measure of your product or service?

Scripture: Can I justify wicked scales and a bag of deceptive weights? (Micah 6:11).

Today's Thought: In an era of downsizing businesses, with the focus on cutting costs, it may also be tempting to cut corners with our products and services. And, unless we have directly cheated a customer, we might even believe that we are following Christian teaching about frugality and wise stewardship by making the most from our investment.

However, any time we fall short of fully serving a customer, or we provide anything less than our best product or service, we have used, in effect, "wicked scales." Any time we fail to fill a cup of coffee, or knowingly ship a product that is not first-rate, or don't make our best effort on behalf of a client, we have measured with deceptive weights.

When we give our best to our customers every day, God will bless our endeavors.

God will not bless such a business. In fact, He warns that "you will eat, but you will not be satisfied. . . . You will try to remove . . . but you will not preserve" (Micah 6:14).

When we give our best, in full measure, to our customers every day, God will bless our endeavors, and we will dwell "in the midst of a fruitful field" (7:14).

Differing weights are an abomination to the LORD, and a false scale is not good (Proverbs 20:23).

Have you clearly communicated your business vision to your staff?

Scripture: Then the LORD answered me and said, "Record the vision and inscribe it on tablets, that the one who reads it may run" (Habakkuk 2:2).

Today's Thought: Dallas Seminary professor Howard Hendricks offers this simple definition of leadership: "Look behind you. If no one is following, you're not leading, you're just taking a walk." As business owners and managers, if we have failed to adequately communicate our corporate vision to our staff, we should not be surprised when they don't follow our lead.

When the entire team embraces a vision, they will begin to run with greater enthusiasm, unity, effectiveness, and purpose.

Are you leading your company, or just taking a walk? Do you have a well-conceived vision that is in writing and clearly communicated to each individual in the organization? Managers must accept the responsibility for ensuring that every team member understands the mission, vision, and direction of the company. And then team leaders must practice what they preach, putting the vision into action that others can emulate.

When the entire team embraces a vision, they will begin to run with greater enthusiasm, unity, effectiveness, and purpose. Service will improve, customers will soon notice the increased energy and focus of your staff, and sales and profits will increase.

Teach a righteous man, and he will increase his learning (Proverbs 9:9).

Do you own your business or does it belong to your creditors?

Scripture: Will not your creditors rise up suddenly, and those who collect from you awaken? Indeed, you will become plunder for them (Habakkuk 2:7).

Today's Thought: Although the Bible does not prohibit borrowing, the Scriptures caution us about the use of credit because of the obligation it creates and the subservient position it places us in relative to our creditors. Still, many businesspeople believe that they need to borrow funds to expand their business, meet current expenses, or obtain financing for capital expenditures.

Before you sign a pledge, consider each debt carefully. Ask yourself these questions: If every loan were called in today, how would I honor my commitments? Do I have the ability to pay all my outstanding obligations? If the amount you owe is greater than the value of the underlying assets, the answer is probably "no."

> **Creditors have a way of rising up suddenly at the worst possible moment.**

If you would not be able to pay off your debts in the event they were called, you are overextended. Take caution: Creditors have a way of rising up suddenly at the worst possible moment. If they do, you will find that you don't own your own business—it belongs to your creditors.

He who is surety for a stranger will surely suffer for it, but he who hates going surety is safe (Proverbs 11:15).

Do you know how your employees are doing?

Scripture: Know well the condition of your flocks, and pay attention to your herds; for riches are not forever (Proverbs 27:23–24).

Today's Thought: Just as a shepherd depends on the quality of his sheep for his livelihood, business owners rely on their employees to provide good customer service, put in an honest day's work, and care for the assets of the company. If your employees are dissatisfied, how well will they serve your customers?

Employees who feel valued will respond with their best performance.

Pay attention to employee morale. One good indicator is a cheerful countenance. Do your employees exude a positive attitude toward you and each other? Do they greet customers warmly and pleasantly? Do they follow through to make sure the job is done right? Do your customers walk out the door feeling they have been well served?

Complacency can be deadly, especially when business is good. Don't spend too much time in your office. Get out and see how your staff is doing. Model a positive attitude and follow up with direct feedback and praise. Employees who feel valued will respond with their best performance.

Happy employees lead to satisfied customers, and satisfied customers will make your business grow.

A joyful heart makes a cheerful face, but when the heart is sad, the spirit is broken (Proverbs 15:13).

When major problems hit your business, are you direct with your staff?

Scripture: Then I said to them, "You see the bad situation we are in" (Nehemiah 2:17).

Today's Thought: When adversity strikes your business, be open and honest with your staff. Explain the situation and communicate your resolve to find a solution—together. After all, it's not just you or the company that is suffering.

Outline the problem in a way that everyone can understand and discuss possible solutions. Solicit input and ideas from others, and ask each member of your staff for help. Clarify roles and responsibilities in the recovery effort, and emphasize the importance of communication and teamwork.

> **When adversity strikes your business, be open and honest with your staff.**

When everyone understands the problem—and what they can do to help—they will be able to pitch in and work together to fix the mess. If you're open and honest about the problem, you'll be amazed at the teamwork and camaraderie that results.

A friend loves at all times, and a brother is born for adversity (Proverbs 17:17).

Is your place of business appealing to customers?

Scripture: Know well the condition of your flocks, and pay attention to your herds; for riches are not forever (Proverbs 27:23–24).

Today's Thought: Take stock of your place of business. Are you showing your best face to your customers? Nobody likes to shop in a run-down store or walk into a messy office. And a dilapidated warehouse or manufacturing plant raises questions about the quality of the products being shipped out the door. When customers walk through your doors, are they impressed or appalled?

Find some low-cost ways to make your business more attractive to customers.

Take time to walk around your establishment with a notepad, writing down items that need to be cleaned up. Take down clutter from walls, wash the windows, and make sure that the floors are clean and the hallways and aisles are clear. Remove old files to storage and get rid of equipment and desks that aren't being used.

Find some low-cost ways to make your business more attractive to customers. Put up a fresh coat of paint. Get the carpets cleaned. Take pride in your place of business and you'll be amazed at the positive response from your customers.

Nor does a crown endure to all generations (Proverbs 27:24).

Are you keeping your customers satisfied?

Scripture: Know well the condition of your flocks, and pay attention to your herds; for riches are not forever (Proverbs 27:23–24).

Today's Thought: A wise shepherd understands the needs of his sheep for good pasture, fresh water, and protection from harm. In business, your customers' needs are not always so obvious. Don't make the mistake of thinking that just because they aren't complaining, they are happy and satisfied.

In today's marketplace, customers will go where their needs are being satisfied.

To understand what your customers want and need from you, there's no substitute for direct feedback. Take time to call your customers, not only to ascertain their current level of satisfaction, but to see what new products or services they desire. Listen to your customers' concerns, and develop an organized method to meet their needs.

If your clientel is mostly walk-in, such as in a restaurant or retail shop, get out front and mingle with your customers. Ask for their honest feedback, then act on their recommendations and suggestions. Be alert for any new items or services they request.

In today's marketplace, customers will go where their needs are being satisfied. Don't fall asleep on the job and let your competitors take away your best customers.

A little folding of your hands to rest—and your poverty will come in like a vagabond (Proverbs 6:10–11).

Are you involved in conflicts at work?

Scripture: Then Abram said to Lot, "Please let there be no strife between you and me, nor between my herdsman and your herdsmen, for we are brothers" (Genesis 13:8).

Today's Thought: Are you at odds with others at work? Do some of your coworkers rub you the wrong way? How do you handle colleagues with whom it is difficult to get along? The apostle Paul says, "If possible, so far as it depends on you, be at peace with all men" (Romans 12:18). It might help to view your coworkers as members of the family. As with family, you might have your differences, but you work them out in a spirit of brotherhood and cooperation. After all, the workplace is really no place for engaging in personal contests and arguments.

When you focus the discussion on solutions rather than problems, it's easier to keep in mind the ultimate goals.

Instead of allowing disagreements to become personal and boil out of control, focus your attention and mind on the specific work-related issue underlying the conflict. Identify the problem, ponder possible solutions, and then determine the best answer to address the obstacle.

When you focus the discussion on solutions rather than problems, it's easier to keep in mind the ultimate goals: improving relationships and building your business.

When a man's ways are pleasing to the LORD, He makes even his enemies to be at peace with him (Proverbs 16:7).

Do you expect business success to come quickly?

Scripture: The LORD your God will clear away these nations before you little by little; you will not be able to put an end to them quickly (Deuteronomy 7:22).

Today's Thought: Only occasionally will a major stroke of fortune or insight bring great success quickly. Most of the time, business success comes only after putting together a lot of little details that add up to a larger whole. Watch the small steps, like the prompt return of phone calls to customers, packing each order securely, being courteous at the front desk, or serving meals hot and fresh in your restaurant.

It is the small steps taken consistently that generate repeat business.

Small tasks done well add up to a successful project. Projects done well add up to business success. It is the small steps taken consistently that generate repeat business.

Sweat the small stuff and do it right, and your business will grow—as will its good reputation.

Do you see a man skilled in his work? He will stand before kings (Proverbs 22:29).

Are coworkers getting your goat and making you mad?

Scripture: Be reconciled to your brother, and then come and present your offering (Matthew 5:24).

Today's Thought: Coworkers are to be considered as our brothers and sisters. When we experience conflict with coworkers, God expects us to be the peacemaker. Always be open to the possibility that you might be wrong. When you are, be quick to repent and apologize.

Coworkers are to be considered as our brothers and sisters.

When you believe others have wronged you, don't let time go by before you go to them directly and privately. Then, calmly and clearly express your concern. Request any change of behavior or attitude you believe is essential.

Remember to listen carefully for feedback and endeavor to resolve the issues completely and constructively. Both teamwork and morale will increase. Your workplace will become more enjoyable as God's love shines through you.

A gentle answer turns away wrath, but a harsh word stirs up anger (Proverbs 15:1).

Are all your words at work honoring to God?

Scripture: Let no unwholesome word proceed from your mouth, but only such a word as is good for edification according to the need of the moment, that it may give grace to those who hear (Ephesians 4:29).

Today's Thought: When you speak to your staff or a colleague, is every word appropriate and gracious, or do people walk away feeling trampled? Here are a few guidelines to make sure that your words always "give grace to those who hear."

First and foremost, be honest. Telling the truth establishes your credibility and makes you a person that others can trust.

Second, speak the truth in love. Be careful not to use judgmental statements or attacking words that may allow you to let off steam but are neither helpful nor appreciated by others. Make sure that what you say is instructive and helpful.

> **When you must correct a worker take on the attitude of a coach, giving guidance and encouragement.**

When you must correct an employee, do so gently. Take on the attitude of a coach, giving guidance and encouragement.

When every word you speak is honest, encouraging, and gently instructive, you will motivate workers to give their best efforts and serve your customers more effectively.

The tongue of the wise makes knowledge acceptable, but the mouth of fools spouts folly (Proverbs 15:2).

As a believing Christian, would you enter into a business partnership with a non-Christian?

Scripture: Do not be unequally yoked together with unbelievers. For what fellowship has righteousness and lawlessness? (2 Corinthians 6:14 NKJV).

Today's Thought: While this verse is often used in referring to a marriage commitment, it also applies to a business partnership. When two oxen of unequal strength are yoked together, the pair will travel in a circle. Regardless of how attractive a business deal may appear, do not enter into a partnership with a non-Christian.

Do not enter into a partnership with a non-Christian.

Also resist the temptation to become a business partner as a witnessing opportunity. "Missionary partnerships" don't work any better than does "missionary dating." Experience reveals it is often the Christian who is dragged down rather than his or her partner being raised up. Witness first; then consider a partnership only when the person comes to Christ. Ignore this piece of biblical wisdom and your business will suffer.

Better is a little with the fear of the LORD than great treasure and turmoil with it (Proverbs 15:16).

Do you operate your business seven days a week?

Scripture: Observe the sabbath day to keep it holy, as the LORD your God commanded you. Six days you shall labor and do all your work (Deuteronomy 5:12–13).

Today's Thought: With the rise of on-line banking, on-line shopping, and the continual push for more convenience, the temptation is strong for businesses to operate 24/7; that is, twenty-four hours a day, seven days a week. But that's not what God intended. He designed life to be cyclical and for our bodies to require rest. Studies have shown that lack of adequate rest contributes to heart attacks, strokes, and other medical difficulties. When we insist on working seven days a week, except for unusual circumstances, such as needing to pull a cow out of a ditch or responding to a fire, we are destined to burn out.

Keep the Sabbath, and keep working as God intended.

If we ignore God's commandment to rest on the Sabbath, our bodies and minds will gradually begin to fail. Our work will eventually suffer, and if we become disabled or die, we will be unable to work at all. Just as God chose to rest after Creation, so should we.

Keep the Sabbath, and keep working as God intended.

Then you will walk in your way securely, and your foot will not stumble (Proverbs 3:23).

Do you keep your employees informed about the business?

Scripture: No longer do I call you slaves; for the slave does not know what his master is doing; but I have called you friends, for all things that I have heard from My Father I have made known to you (John 15:15).

Today's Thought: Informed employees are usually more effective. When you share important and appropriate information with your staff, they will better understand how their jobs fit into the scope of the business and how their individual efforts can contribute to improving the quality of your products and services.

Develop a habit of sharing your knowledge every day.

Consider Jesus' example of open and forthright communication. Develop a habit of sharing your knowledge every day. Make a list of important topics to cover, and then create a consistent flow of good communication regarding your business each day.

Another great thing about communication is that it's a two-way street. As you open up with your employees, they will open up with you and all kinds of great ideas will surface. Over time, you will be amazed by the improvement in staff performance as each person becomes more involved in the success of your business.

Where there is no guidance, the people fall (Proverbs 11:14).

Is any of your business equipment outdated?

Scripture: If the ax is dull and he does not sharpen its edge, then he must exert more strength. Wisdom has the advantage of giving success (Ecclesiastes 10:10).

Today's Thought: Too often we allow the tools of our trade to grow dull or become outdated. This creates frustration for everyone. None of us like to work harder and harder only to achieve fewer and fewer results.

Consider making a list of all your equipment and then checking each piece to see if improvement is needed. Evaluate your cash registers, your computer hard drives and software packages, your copiers and fax machines, your plant machinery. Ask yourself, "Is each ax sharp?" Time has a way of dulling even the best and sharpest tools.

Time has a way of dulling even the best and sharpest tools.

The improvements you make and the axes you sharpen in your business tool chest will make each staff member more effective and every day more profitable. Remember, the pros use only the best.

Know well the condition of your flocks [business], and pay attention to your herds; for riches are not forever (Proverbs 27:23–24).

Have you allowed yourself to become dull in your job?

Scripture: If the ax is dull and he does not sharpen its edge, then he must exert more strength. Wisdom has the advantage of giving success (Ecclesiastes 10:10).

Today's Thought: If you've ever tried to cut wood with a dull ax, you know how much effort is required. But as soon as the blade is sharpened, the work can proceed with much less exertion. The secret lies in knowing when to stop and sharpen the blade. The same principle holds true at work. If you're stuck in a pattern of doing the same things every day, and you feel as though you're becoming dull, perhaps it's time to stop and "sharpen your ax."

It always pays to stop long enough to sharpen the ax.

Sign up for a business seminar, read a business book or magazine, or attend a trade show. Take decisive action to restore a sharp edge to your productivity. Stay motivated and accept no excuses for not increasing your efficiency and effectiveness.

Often, we tell ourselves that we don't have enough time for additional training or reading because we have too much work to do. But it always pays to stop long enough to sharpen the ax.

Iron sharpens iron, so one man sharpens another (Proverbs 27:17).

Is all or part of your business failing to prosper?

Scripture: I have come looking for fruit on this fig tree without finding any. Cut it down! Why does it even use up the ground? (Luke 13:7).

Today's Thought: In business, there is time to make some hard decisions about when to cut our losses on a project. Not everything we try, no matter how well conceived, thought out, and executed, will accomplish our goals. We must determine when it is wise to stop pouring more energy and resources into a project that just isn't working out.

Establish a time frame in which to achieve your goals and set a maximum dollar loss you can afford. If you don't, unsuccessful initiatives have a way of continuing on and on and acquiring a life of their own. They become like a friend of mine's definition of his boat: "A hole in the water lined with wood into which I pour money."

> Not everything we try, no matter how well conceived, thought out, and executed, will accomplish our goals.

He who tills his land will have plenty of bread, but he who pursues vain things lacks sense (Proverbs 12:11).

23

Is your business built on a strong foundation for long-term success?

Scripture: Therefore everyone who hears these words of Mine, and acts upon them, may be compared to a wise man, who built his house upon the rock. And the rain descended, and the floods came, and the winds blew, and burst against that house; and yet it did not fall, for it had been founded upon the rock (Matthew 7:24–25).

Today's Thought: In today's economy, many businesses borrow extensively to finance new expansion, increase inventory, purchase new equipment, and enter new markets.

While the sun shines, interest rates are low, and business is good, servicing the debt may be manageable, and you might be tempted to increase borrowing to accelerate your business plan.

Keep your outstanding obligations to a minimum and your business will be built on solid rock.

Inevitably, however, the winds and rains will come, the economy will hit a down cycle, and business will slow. Your foundation will be tested. Are you prepared? If your business is not built on solid rock—especially financially—you may find all your hard work washed away before you can respond.

Use the good times to pay down your debt. Keep your outstanding obligations to a minimum and your business will be built on solid rock.

The badgers are not mighty folk, yet they make their houses in the rocks (Proverbs 30:26).

What kind of example do you set for your coworkers?

Scripture: And I also applied myself to the work on this wall; we did not buy any land, and all my servants were gathered there for the work (Nehemiah 5:16).

Today's Thought: When Nehemiah was appointed governor of Judah, he had every right to receive taxes and food offerings from the people. But he refused to take advantage of his privileged position and chose instead to help the people rebuild the walls of Jerusalem. Not only did he get his own hands dirty, but he put his servants and attendants to work as well.

On the job, are you a model of integrity and hard work? Are you willing to pitch in to get the job done, or do you take advantage of your position? Are you accepting any unreasonable perks or favors? Take an honest look in the mirror. Would you want your staff to follow your example?

> Your positive work ethic will increase productivity—and success will follow.

If you're a leader, your business or department will reflect your values and your staff will live by your example. Set a high standard, keep your nose to the grindstone, and lead with integrity. Your positive work ethic will increase productivity—and success will follow.

It is by his deeds that a lad distinguishes himself if his conduct is pure and right (Proverbs 20:11).

Do you gossip against your boss?

Scripture: Let all who are under the yoke as slaves regard their own masters as worthy of all honor so that the name of God and our doctrine may not be spoken against (I Timothy 6:1).

Today's Thought: When coworkers speak against the boss, don't join in. Follow the old adage, "If you can't say something nice, don't say anything at all." Not only will it keep you out of trouble, it is honoring to your boss. If you do say anything, your comments should be positive, supportive statements that balance a situation.

Cutting down the boss only destroys morale for everyone, including you.

Cutting down the boss only destroys morale for everyone. The workplace takes on a negative atmosphere, and you begin to believe all the exaggerations you hear.

If slaves who occupied the lowest state imaginable are commanded to honor their masters, then surely we, as employees, should honor those who supervise us. If you do have a complaint, sit down with your supervisor and calmly discuss the issue. In this way you can be part of the solution, not part of the problem.

He who despises his neighbor lacks sense, but a man of understanding keeps silent (Proverbs 11:12).

When resolving issues at work, do you stick to the facts or jump to conclusions?

Scripture: But refuse foolish and ignorant speculations, knowing that they produce quarrels (2 Timothy 2:23).

Today's Thought: When issues arise at work, are you tempted to argue without first gathering all the facts? When others disagree, do you become defensive, entrenched, and inflexible? The Bible calls that foolishness.

Don't jump to conclusions. Focus first on understanding the situation. Make sure that all the facts are out on the table. If the issue is controversial, get more than one perspective. Ask probing questions to establish what is true and what is merely speculation.

By withholding judgment and seeking first to fully understand, you build trust with your coworkers and gain their confidence in your decisions.

By withholding judgment and seeking first to fully understand, you build trust with your coworkers and gain their confidence in your decisions. It's easy to jump to conclusions; it takes discipline and self-control to sort through all the facts before responding.

Usually, when all the facts are clearly presented and understood, a distinct course of action will emerge. If you haven't burned your bridges in the process, you can now move forward or back with confidence. Either way, your decisions will be more balanced, correct, and fair, and your business will ultimately run more smoothly.

The glory of kings is to search out a matter (Proverbs 25:2).

Do you accomplish the urgent at the expense of the important in your business?

Scripture: "For I know the plans that I have for you," declares the LORD, "plans for welfare and not for calamity to give you a future and a hope" (Jeremiah 29:11).

Today's Thought: If the Lord plans, so must you and I. Determining key objectives and planning sound strategies make a major difference in the success of a business. If you don't have objectives or a strategy, the daily grind will take over and your business will stay stuck in the mud of mediocrity.

Each day, write on your calendar one objective that will make a difference that day.

Each day, write on your calendar one objective that will make a difference that day; then focus on getting the task done. Accept no excuses from yourself. Day by day, you will see real progress in your business.

Jesus never accepted the urgent as a substitute for the truly important and neither should we.

Like a city that is broken into and without walls is a man who has no control over his spirit (Proverbs 25:28).

Have you borrowed money to finance your business?

Scripture: The rich rules over the poor, and the borrower becomes the lender's slave (Proverbs 22:7).

Today's Thought: When a business borrows money, the lender usually requires the signing of a loan covenant agreement, along with a promissory note that says the business will pay off the debt. Sometimes the bank even asks for a personal guarantee from the owner of the business.

Loan covenants are long, detailed documents full of fine print. Often they place restrictions on the borrower, such as controlling their extension of credit to customers, limiting management salaries, restricting capital spending, and regulating other business decisions. A primary lender can even dictate

When you borrow from the bank, you become a servant to the banker.

the order in which other creditors will be paid in the event of insolvency. If a borrower violates any part of a loan covenant, the banker can declare the loan in default and require immediate repayment. Just as Solomon warns in the Book of Proverbs, "the borrower becomes the lender's slave."

It might be necessary for your business to borrow money in order to accomplish your objectives, but don't make such a decision unwisely. Remember, when you borrow from the bank, you become a servant to the banker.

If you have nothing with which to pay, why should he take your bed from under you? (Proverbs 22:27).

Do you hire only young workers, overlooking someone because he or she seems too old?

Scripture: Older men are to be temperate, dignified, sensible, sound in faith, in love, in perseverance (Titus 2:2).

Today's Thought: What employer wouldn't give an arm and a leg for these attributes in a worker? When hiring, consider older, more experienced workers to stabilize a young workforce. McDonalds learned this years ago and specifically recruited retired workers.

When hiring, consider older, more experienced workers to stabilize a young workforce.

Mature staff can coach, mentor, and be an example to younger workers—and make them more productive. You may pay a little more in wages, but you will capture invaluable experience that can directly affect your bottom line.

Remember, Moses was eighty when he was just getting started. Use experience to beef up your profits.

Iron sharpens iron, so one man sharpens another (Proverbs 27:17).

Do you manage your company's cash flow by not paying your bills on time?

Scripture: Do not withhold good from those to whom it is due, when it is in your power to do it. Do not say to your neighbor, "Go, and come back, and tomorrow I will give it," when you have it with you (Proverbs 3:27–28).

Today's Thought: It can be tempting not to pay your bills on time when you know that a vendor will not immediately call to collect. And when your own collections are slow, it's even easier to let your payables slide for a while. Some would argue that this is good cash management, but withholding payment is never pleasing to God.

If you want to be obedient to Scripture, follow through on paying invoices within the prescribed terms. Don't string your suppliers along. If you can't meet their requirements, ask to change the terms of sale. But don't make a promise you don't intend to keep.

When you've proven yourself reliable, your vendor will want to meet your needs.

When you pay on time, you enhance your position to bargain for the best prices, ask for increased service, and negotiate the best terms. When you've proven yourself reliable, your vendor will want to perform and meet your needs.

There is one who withholds what is justly due, but it results only in want (Proverbs 11:24).

Do you act like you have all the answers and don't need advice?

Scripture: A poor, yet wise lad is better than an old and foolish king who no longer knows how to receive instruction (Ecclesiastes 4:13).

Today's Thought: As our experience grows and we move up the management ladder, it's easy to start thinking that we see things more clearly than our colleagues and subordinates and that we don't really need or want any new input.

> **Encouraging the counsel of others builds teamwork and may help you avoid costly mistakes.**

Nothing could be more dangerous in business than the attitude that you alone have all the answers. Instead, make it a priority to seek the counsel of others. Coworkers, even those with limited experience, can often alert you to major problems. Those who are closest to the action can broaden your perspective of what is happening and may also have good suggestions for what can be done.

When ideas come forward, be thankful and encouraging. If the ideas are useful, give proper credit, and implement the suggestions. If the ideas are not feasible, explain why they can't be used, but invite the other person to keep offering input. Encouraging the counsel of others builds teamwork and may help you avoid costly mistakes.

Through presumption comes nothing but strife, but with those who receive counsel is wisdom (Proverbs 13:10).

Are you impartial in your decisions to hire and promote women?

Scripture: Then you will discern righteousness and justice and equity and every good course (Proverbs 2:9).

Today's Thought: Regardless of your personal perspective on the role of women in the workplace, your responsibility as an owner or manager is to be impartial. For your business to be successful, you should seek to fill each position with the best talent available, regardless of gender. It only makes sense, then, women would be hired, trained, and promoted on an equal basis with men.

Many women work to help balance the family budget, to support themselves, or, as single parents, to support themselves and their children. Yet even though women have played an increasingly prominent role in the workforce since the end of World War II, they still are often not treated equally with men.

> Impartial hiring and promotion decisions will strengthen your workforce and make everyone more productive.

Creating an equitable workplace starts with creating a well-written job description and having a clear understanding of the qualifications necessary for success in each position. Then look for employees whose interests, aptitudes, and personality fit the job and the climate of your company.

Impartial hiring and promotion decisions will strengthen your workforce, make everyone more productive, and increase your profits.

To show partiality is not good (Proverbs 28:21).

Do you accept correction and discipline from your boss?

Scripture: For whom the LORD loves He reproves, even as a father, the son in whom he delights (Proverbs 3:12).

Today's Thought: Accepting correction is never easy. Because we're human, our natural response is to make excuses and defend ourselves. Just look at Adam and Eve in the Garden of Eden. If we're wise, however, we will learn from our mistakes, accept discipline and reproof, and improve our performance.

The best way to respond to correction is with courtesy and professionalism. When criticized, avoid being defensive; don't lash back. Instead, listen to the comments carefully and accept the information graciously. When you are wrong, quickly admit your error and resolve to correct your work. Thank your supervisor for being willing to point out areas in your performance that need improvement.

If you learn to accept constructive criticism, your performance will improve.

When you display a humble attitude, your boss will be amazed and impressed. Willingness to learn and to adjust your work habits will increase your value to the company, and your job satisfaction will increase as well. Although it's never easy to submit to discipline and correction, if you learn to accept constructive criticism, your performance will improve.

Poverty and shame will come to him who neglects discipline, but he who regards reproof will be honored (Proverbs 13:18).

Have you been satisfied with an apparent victory, stopping short of complete success?

Scripture: And it came about when Israel became strong, that they put the Canaanites to forced labor, but they did not drive them out completely (Judges 1:28).

Today's Thought: When God delivered victory to the Israelites, he instructed them to drive the Canaanites completely out of the Promised Land. But instead of finishing the task, the army stopped short of full possession—and the Canaanites continued to plague Israel for years to come.

Loose ends can plague your business as well. There's an old adage that goes "Well begun is half done." It takes persistence, discipline, and hard work to finish the job. Even when a task at work seems complete and looks successful, make sure you have followed through diligently in every respect. Don't waste a major effort by failing to wrap up the last 3 percent of the job.

> Following through completely will distinguish you from others, help you maintain your victories, and improve profitability.

Go the extra mile. Finish filing those documents, write that follow-up report, inspect the final product, ask your customer for feedback. Following through completely will distinguish you from others, help you maintain your victories, and improve your overall performance and profitability.

Poor is he who works with a negligent hand, but the hand of the diligent makes rich (Proverbs 10:4).

Have you ever been afraid to provide moral leadership in your business?

Scripture: And Aaron said, "Do not let the anger of my lord burn; you know the people yourself, that they are prone to evil" (Exodus 32:22).

Today's Thought: When Aaron failed to keep the Israelites from sin and they built the golden calf at the foot of Mt. Sinai, the results were catastrophic. As a consequence of Aaron's lack of moral leadership, three thousand Israelites were killed.

In business, the effects of immorality may not be life or death, but they are nevertheless negative. Compromising the truth may cost you a valued customer; lying on an expense report may cost someone his job; sexual harassment may result in legal action; and failure to comply with safety regulations or equal employment laws can result in fines and sanctions.

Stop all wrongdoing in its tracks and your business will remain on solid ground.

In today's workplace, our principles will be challenged by colleagues who cut corners, make inappropriate comments and compromises, or engage in unethical behavior. Our standards must be clear and our behavior consistent.

Most problems in business start small, then mushroom. If you nip potential problems in the bud, establish clear standards of propriety, and stop all wrongdoing in its tracks, your business will remain on solid ground.

A righteous man hates falsehood, but a wicked man acts disgustingly and shamefully (Proverbs 13:5).

Are you secretly hoping someone else will follow through in an area for which you are responsible?

Scripture: Arise! For this matter is your responsibility, but we will be with you; be courageous and act (Ezra 10:4).

Today's Thought: You cannot wait for others to act when the responsibility is yours. Follow through with customers' orders and service requests. Too often we say "I'm doing the best I can" or "It's the supplier's fault for the mix-up." By shifting the blame, we think we have washed our hands of the problem.

But the fact remains—your responsibility is your responsibility, period. Accept it, then act on it. Don't offer excuses for any service or quality problem or for not meeting customer commitments. Intervene personally if necessary. Go out of your way to correct the problem instead of asking the customer to bear the consequences. Your customers will not only be delighted, but they will come back for more of your business.

Don't offer excuses for any services or quality problems.

He also who is slack in his work is brother to him who destroys (Proverbs 18:9).

37

Have you ever told your boss that a problem was not your fault?

Scripture: Arise! For this matter is your responsibility, but we will be with you; be courageous and act (Ezra 10:4).

Today's Thought: When asked the reason for his team's defeat one day, a wise baseball manager snapped, "Excuses don't win ball games." How true, and yet how often we try to cover our losses with great explanations. Sometimes we act as though a bad result plus a good story equals a favorable outcome. Clearly, this is faulty math. Excuses and rationalizations never substitute for purposeful action and follow-through.

> Accept responsibility, allow yourself to be held accountable, and establish a habit of action in every circumstance.

The next time you fall short on the job, don't try to vindicate yourself with excuses. Instead, simply accept the criticism, apologize, and take the necessary steps to correct the problem. Redouble your efforts and work to remove any obstacles blocking you from success.

As you accept responsibility, allow yourself to be held accountable, and establish a habit of action in every circumstance, your boss will take notice, your value to the company will increase, and your opportunities for promotion and better salary increases will expand.

A wise son accepts his father's discipline, but a scoffer does not listen to rebuke (Proverbs 13:1).

Is your staff focused on key business issues?

Scripture: Where there is no vision, the people are unrestrained (Proverbs 29:18).

Today's Thought: As managers, we see the big picture, we understand the key issues facing our business or department, and we want our staff to comply with our directions. But unless we communicate effectively with our employees, they may not be focused on what's really important.

Make sure you have clearly outlined the vision for your business or department. Don't assume that everyone already knows and understands. Clarify your goals and explain how you will measure success. Help team members see how their jobs fit into the big picture, and then affirm and validate their importance and their performance at every opportunity.

When a business has a clear vision and goals, everyone can work together for better productivity.

Your words and actions should support and reinforce the vision. Lead by example and demonstrate how excellent work helps the entire organization.

When mistakes are made, explain how the problems affect the overall goals of the business and then collaborate with your team to establish corrective measures. When a business has a clear vision and goals, everyone can work together for better productivity.

Commit your works to the LORD, and your plans will be established (Proverbs 16:3).

Do you hire only employees who are just like you?

Scripture: For just as we have many members in one body and all the members do not have the same function, so we, who are many, are one body in Christ, and individually members one of another (Romans 12:4–5).

Today's Thought: To be truly effective a business requires a diversity of gifted individuals. Even though you might be more comfortable around people with similar personalities, gifts, and interests, if you hire only people who are just like you, your business will become unbalanced.

As you evaluate your company's needs, look for staff members who will shore up your weaknesses, even though they might be weak in your areas of strength. For example, if you are a visionary who likes to explore ideas and concepts, hire someone who loves to follow up with the details, even though you may not always see eye to eye. Carefully identify the skills and competencies required for each position, then hire individuals who closely fit the bill.

> **Hiring a diverse team of qualified workers will boost productivity and improve your business.**

Balance your team by thoughtfully and prayerfully matching up the needed skills with a variety of gifted individuals. Hiring a diverse team of qualified workers will boost productivity and improve your business.

A wise man is strong, and a man of knowledge increases power (Proverbs 24:5).

Are you fearful of your competitors?

Scripture: And David said to Saul, "Let no man's heart fail on account of him; your servant will go and fight with this Philistine" (1 Samuel 17:32).

Today's Thought: When David went out to face Goliath, he didn't spend a lot of time sizing up the competition and exposing himself to intimidation. Instead, he reviewed his earlier successes against the lion and the bear, took stock of his available resources, then ran out to join the battle, armed with appropriate and familiar weapons and with the purpose clearly in mind.

If you're facing a formidable foe in business, don't panic. Maximize your strengths and take advantage of your competitor's weaknesses. Every business has its weak points. Are your competitors big and strong, but slow and inflexible? Are there chinks in their armor, gaps in their defenses?

When you're committed to success through persistence and hard work, the victory will be yours.

Look for openings and opportunities, then devise and execute strategies to exploit your best advantage. Often, the best plans are the simplest. As you implement your ideas, gains will be made, successes will be clear, and your confidence will increase.

David believed in the mission and won the battle. Likewise, when you're committed to success through persistence and hard work, the victory will be yours.

He who listens to me shall live securely, and shall be at ease from the dread of evil (Proverbs 1:33).

Do you attempt to accomplish big jobs all at once?

Scripture: The LORD spoke to Joshua the son of Nun, Moses' servant, saying, . . . "Every place on which the sole of your foot treads, I have given it to you, just as I spoke to Moses" (Joshua 1:1, 3).

Today's Thought: When Israel entered Canaan, God promised to help Joshua and the people subdue the land. Still, they needed fifteen years to complete their conquest, even with God's help. We can learn an important business lesson from this story: Large tasks are usually accomplished by a series of small steps.

Focus on winning the small battles in order to win the war.

Under God's direction, Joshua planned each attack carefully, sizing up the enemy, devising a strategy, then finishing off the battle. One at a time each Canaanite city was captured, which allowed the sons of Israel to take possession of the land without being overextended.

In business, the objectives are the same. Break down your large goals into manageable action steps and you will be amazed at how steadily you can accomplish your objectives. Analyze your situation. Plan carefully. Finish key tasks completely before moving on to the next target. Focus on winning the small battles in order to win the war.

Every prudent man acts with knowledge, but a fool displays folly (Proverbs 13:16).

Have you ever said, "That's not my job!"?

Scripture: Bear one another's burdens, and thus fulfill the law of Christ (Galatians 6:2).

Today's Thought: We demonstrate the servant heart of Jesus when we lend a hand to coworkers who need assistance. Obviously we're not to take over their jobs or allow them to shirk their responsibilities through laziness, but it's appropriate to share the load and bear one another's burdens, especially when it benefits your customers or advances the mission of the organization. A true team player never says, "That's not my job."

To give us an example of how to live, Jesus was willing to get his hands dirty, humbling himself to do the work of a servant by washing the disciples' feet. As you focus on helping your coworkers, be willing to stoop down and do what's necessary.

> **By developing an attitude of service, you can help the entire organization win.**

Managers, help out employees by restocking shelves or returning phone calls. Employees, be willing to cross-train in other areas to make yourself more versatile. By developing an attitude of service, you can help the entire organization win.

Do not withhold good from those to whom it is due, when it is in your power to do it (Proverbs 3:27).

Are you frustrated with not receiving more responsibility at work?

Scripture: His master said to him, "Well done, good and faithful slave; you were faithful with a few things, I will put you in charge of many things, enter into the joy of your master" (Matthew 25:21).

Today's Thought: If you want more responsibility at work, first make sure that you are following through completely on all current assignments and duties. Do a good job with every task entrusted to you. Take advantage of every opportunity to demonstrate your value to the company and don't consider any job beneath your dignity. Often it's the little things that make the biggest difference.

In everything, maintain a cheerful disposition and a confident, optimistic outlook.

Be on time for work every day, keep appointments diligently, and return phone calls promptly. Complete reports and other paperwork thoroughly and timely, come prepared for meetings, and don't leave little requests from your boss unfinished. Above all, don't complain. In everything, maintain a cheerful disposition and a confident, optimistic outlook.

If you establish an attitude of faithfulness, persistence, and loyalty, it won't take long for your boss to notice your efforts and reward you with increased responsibility.

Do you see a man skilled in his work? He will stand before kings; he will not stand before obscure men (Proverbs 22:29).

Do you have a succession plan in place for your business?

Scripture: Now when David reached old age, he made his son Solomon king over Israel (1 Chronicles 23:1).

Today's Thought: Many business owners act as if they believe they will live forever here on earth. How else can they explain their failure to develop a succession plan for the future of their companies? Unfortunately, as the old saying goes, "Failure to plan is planning to fail." If you want your business to survive and prosper after you are gone, you need a plan for handing over the reins to your successor.

None of us will stay in the saddle forever. For everyone's benefit, a wise owner plans for retirement well in advance. Can you imagine the infighting that might have taken place had David not named one of his sons to succeed him as king? The people would not have known whom to follow. Confusion would have reigned instead of the wisdom of Solomon.

Make plans and prepare others for the day when you will leave.

Make plans and prepare others for the day when you will leave. You owe it to your business as well as to your successor. Your legacy may depend on how well you plan your departure.

Many are the plans in a man's heart, but the counsel of the LORD, it will stand (Proverbs 19:21).

Are you careful in choosing your business counselors?

Scripture: Then King Rehoboam consulted with the elders who had served his father. . . . But he forsook the counsel of the elders which they had given him, and consulted with the young men who grew up with him and served him (2 Chronicles 10:6, 8).

Today's Thought: When Rehoboam succeeded his father, Solomon, on the throne of Judah, he was wise to consult with experienced counselors. But when he foolishly disregarded their advice, the results were disastrous.

Evaluate every new idea in light of the wisdom of experience.

When seeking direction for your business, surround yourself with senior, well-seasoned mentors whose perspective has been tempered by time. Listen to counselors who will tell you what you need to hear and not just what you want to hear.

Younger counselors often bring fresh, new, creative ideas which can be helpful and energizing, but don't be swayed by your emotions. Evaluate every new idea in light of the wisdom of experience.

When listening to advice, balance the vision, exuberance, and creativity of youth with the levelheaded voice of experience and you will be amazed at how the quality of your decisions improves.

A wise man will hear and increase in learning, and a man of understanding will acquire wise counsel (Proverbs 1:5).

Do you waste time worrying about circumstances you can't control?

Scripture: Therefore do not be anxious for tomorrow; for tomorrow will care for itself. Each day has enough trouble of its own (Matthew 6:34).

Today's Thought: When circumstances go against you and your business is facing adversity, it's time to narrow your focus. That's not to say you should bury your head in the sand, or pretend that everything is rosy when it's not, but when a situation is overwhelming, the wise course of action is to stop and ask yourself what you can change with your available resources.

Focus on small actions that will improve your situation. It's like sailing on the ocean during a major storm. You can't stop the wind or the waves, but you can bail water out of the boat.

You can't stop the wind or the waves, but you can bail water out of the boat.

Don't ignore trouble, but look for positive action you and your staff can take. Commit your ways to God in prayer, and then attack the problem where you can make the most difference. Your cool-headed leadership in times of trouble may very well save the day for your business.

If you are slack in the day of distress, your strength is limited (Proverbs 24:10).

Have you slackened your efforts at work, believing that God will take care of everything?

Scripture: Look at the birds of the air, that they do not sow, neither do they reap, nor gather into barns, and yet your heavenly Father feeds them (Matthew 6:26).

Today's Thought: When we contemplate God's promises to meet our needs, we must be careful not to confuse his admonitions about worry with our responsibility to work diligently. Consider what Jesus says about the birds of the air in Matthew 6. Just because the sparrow doesn't concern itself with sowing, reaping, and gathering doesn't mean it doesn't work hard for its food. Birds don't sit around on fenceposts waiting for seeds to fall into their mouths. Instead, they fly hither and yon, looking for insects, worms, and berries. And out of the bounty of the earth, the Lord supplies their needs.

Birds don't sit around on fenceposts waiting for seeds to fall into their mouths.

In like fashion, our heavenly Father gives fruit to our labors and provides a bountiful harvest of good things. Our responsibility is to seek first his righteousness, commit our plans to his purposes, and work diligently at what he gives us to do. As we're faithful to do our part, God promises to bless our efforts.

How long will you lie down, O sluggard? (Proverbs 6:9).

48

Are you willing to confess your mistakes to your coworkers?

Scripture: Therefore, confess your sins to one another, and pray for one another, so that you may be healed (James 5:16).

Today's Thought: James 5:16 is often quoted to remind us of our need to confess our sins to other believers. The same principle holds true for admitting our errors and mistakes at work. When we're honest about our shortcomings on the job, we benefit in three important ways:

When we openly admit our mistakes and learn from them, others will soon follow our example.

- We lose our fear of looking bad. After all, everyone makes mistakes. We really only look bad when we try to cover them up. Coming clean takes all the pressure off.
- We create opportunities to learn from our mistakes and avoid a repeat performance. When we're open about our errors, we can invite others to give us constructive input to help us learn and grow.
- We gain the respect of coworkers. Often, people know when we have messed up anyway, so why not acknowledge it? Don't let pride stand in the way.

When we openly admit our mistakes and learn from them, others will soon follow our example. You will be amazed by the improvement in company morale and productivity.

He who conceals his transgressions will not prosper, but he who confesses and forsakes them will find compassion (Proverbs 28:13).

49

Are you willing to invest in your greatest asset—your staff?

Scripture: Now this I say, he who sows sparingly shall also reap sparingly; and he who sows bountifully shall also reap bountifully (2 Corinthians 9:6).

Today's Thought: An often overlooked key to productivity is staff training. While business owners are willing to spend money on equipment and inventory, they neglect one of the best investments they can make—in their people. Let's face it, great people are what make great companies go. They are a company's greatest assets.

If you want your company to become more productive, invest in your people.

Start by giving new hires a thorough orientation. Explain your business, your mission, vision, and values. Discuss your products and services and how you want to serve your customers.

Next, help them become familiar with their workstation, show them where office supplies are kept, and explain how all the equipment works. Such instruction may seem basic, but it will pay off in productivity. Encourage them to ask questions, and follow up to make sure they have assimilated all the information.

Training takes time and energy—and yes, it costs money—but it pays huge dividends as well. If you want your company to become more productive, invest in your people.

Give prudence to the naive, to the youth knowledge and discretion. (Proverbs 1:4).

Do you think your memory is so good that you don't need to write things down?

Scripture: "All this," said David, "the LORD made me understand in writing by His hand upon me, all the details of this pattern" (1 Chronicles 28:19).

Today's Thought: No matter how good your memory might be, nobody can remember everything. If you fail to write down important facts or assignments, you are destined to drop the ball sometime and fail to follow through. Creating a "paper trail" helps you keep your bearings and focus your priorities.

Make a habit of taking notes during company meetings and insist that your staff develop the same practice. Emphasize key points, and remind others to write them down. Write down instructions from your boss and give written feedback and suggestions as well.

Putting things in writing helps everyone communicate better.

When a customer expresses a need or makes a request, write it down, along with ideas or instructions for what needs to be done. That way, if you're out of the office or on vacation, coworkers can pick up the slack and serve your customer more efficiently.

Putting things in writing helps everyone communicate better. Developing this important habit will result in happier customers and greater efficiency for your business.

Do not let kindness and truth leave you; bind them around your neck, write them on the tablet of your heart (Proverbs 3:3).

Do you know when to take action and move on?

Scripture: The LORD our God spoke to us at Horeb, saying, "You have stayed long enough at this mountain. Turn and set your journey" (Deuteronomy 1:6–7).

Today's Thought: It's easy to become complacent in business, simply doing the same familiar things day after day. But if we're not careful, before long we can become reluctant to move into new ventures or to undertake new projects. In our rapidly changing global economy, maintaining the status quo is a dangerous mind-set.

Develop a habit of taking action, and watch your business move steadily forward each day.

In every business there is a time to move on, to try new things, to stir up the creative juices and look for new opportunities. Push forward, create some momentum, and insist that your staff follow suit.

Overcome laziness and your reluctance to change. Don't wait until tomorrow to accomplish a task—do it now. Don't let fear of the unknown hold you back. Remember that even though a ship is safest while in harbor, they are built to sail. Set sail with a new idea and see where the winds of change take you. Develop a habit of taking action, and watch your business move steadily forward each day.

She considers a field and buys it; from her earnings she plants a vineyard (Proverbs 31:16).

When a customer calls to complain or to get information, do you answer honestly?

Scripture: You shall know the truth, and the truth shall make you free (John 8:32).

Today's Thought: You've heard it said that honesty is the best policy. But if you make a mistake and a customer calls to complain, do you answer honestly? Customers abhor excuses, especially dishonest ones. If you try to weasel out of your responsibility, you will lose credibility. Instead of trying to get yourself off the hook, admit your shortcomings and apologize to the customer for your failure. Then take the necessary steps to avoid making the same mistake again.

When customers call to confirm delivery dates, do you give them the straight scoop? Whatever you do, don't promise a date you can't meet or give an answer just to get them off the phone. If you manage their expectations honestly in advance, your customers can plan accordingly. But if you fudge to avoid confrontation, they will be even angrier when the truth comes out. Provide honest, accurate answers up front, and you won't have to worry about suffering the consequences later. Your customers will appreciate your honesty and they'll keep coming back.

Your customers will appreciate your honesty and they'll keep coming back.

There is a way which seems right to a man, but its end is the way of death (Proverbs 16:25).

Do you run your business day to day, without much thought to planning?

Scripture: "For I know the plans that I have for you," declares the LORD, "plans for welfare and not for calamity to give you a future and a hope" (Jeremiah 29:11).

Today's Thought: The Lord has a plan for each one of us. He doesn't float from day to day, playing it by ear or making it up as he goes along. He is the God of order, systems, and processes. Of course, we don't have God's ability to see the end from the beginning, but if we want to follow his example by establishing and maintaining order in our businesses, we can still look ahead and make plans.

Establish your plans, and watch your business improve as your goals are achieved.

Take one business quarter as a starting point. Establish three meaningful goals that will have a major impact on your business over the next ninety days. Write them down and communicate them to your staff. When everyone can see the goals and direction of your company, morale will improve, and a sense of purpose will be created, even in difficult circumstances.

Follow God's example, establish your plans, and watch your business improve as your goals are achieved.

Watch the path of your feet, and all your ways will be established (Proverbs 4:26).

Do you pay heed to your boss at work?

Scripture: And when He had finished speaking, He said to Simon, "Put out into the deep water and let down your nets for a catch." And Simon answered and said, "Master, we worked hard all night and caught nothing, but at Your bidding I will let down the nets" (Luke 5:4–5).

Today's Thought: Our earthly bosses may not always be correct, and we may think that we know better, but they have been granted authority over us at work, and we must respond to their guidance.

Notice how Simon Peter answers Jesus. He first explains his view of the situation, but then he willingly submits to Christ's direction. If we're wise, we will follow Peter's example. If you have a disagreement with your boss, discuss your perspective calmly and respectfully. Then, if your boss insists on a particular course of action, you must proceed accordingly.

> Our earthly bosses have been granted authority over us at work, and we must respond to their guidance.

In business, knowledge and experience spells success. That's why effective bosses will be right most of the time. Don't forget, when Simon Peter heeded Christ's advice and lowered the nets, the catch was great!

He who tends the fig tree will eat its fruit; and he who cares for his master will be honored (Proverbs 27:18).

When you introduce an incentive plan, do you get the results you expect?

Scripture: The plans of the diligent lead surely to advantage, but everyone who is hasty comes surely to poverty (Proverbs 21:5).

Today's Thought: A key business principle for managing a staff is that you will get the behavior you reward. If you want to motivate employees to produce specific results, you must connect the proper incentives to the desired outcome. This takes careful planning.

Don't be too quick to change your compensation structure. First, thoroughly analyze the behaviors and results you want from your staff. For example, which is more important for your sales department: gross revenue or margin? If the best indicator of success for your business is gross revenue, tie the commission structure for your sales force to gross sales. On the other hand, if some products are more difficult to sell but are more profitable to the company, consider raising the commission value of these products.

Carefully planning your incentives will lead to greater profitability.

On the manufacturing side, if quality is your main concern, consider tying bonuses or raises to increases in quality. Likewise for productivity. No matter what your priorities are, carefully planning your incentives will lead to greater profitability.

The generous man will be prosperous, and he who waters will himself be watered (Proverbs 11:25).

Do you express irritation to coworkers or show anger at work?

Scripture: For vexation slays the foolish man, and anger kills the simple (Job 5:2).

Today's Thought: When we allow ourselves to become frustrated or angry at work, we harm ourselves more than others. Medical evidence has shown that anger causes health problems, including an increased risk of heart attacks. Also, when we explode with rage, we destroy relationships and damage our ability to work with others.

If you have been offended or wronged by a coworker, ask God for the grace to forgive the other person just as God has forgiven you. Then, if further action is necessary, calmly go to the offender and state your concerns clearly and objectively. Most anger builds up when we fail to take this important step. You may find that your frustration is based on a simple misunderstanding.

> **Replacing anger with constructive action short-circuits the escalation process.**

Work together with your colleague to reach a mutually beneficial resolution. If you approach your coworker with humility, there should be no need for anger or defensiveness in return.

When we replace our frustration with forgiveness and our anger with constructive action, we short-circuit the escalation process. In the end, everyone benefits from a peaceful workplace.

He who is slow to anger is better than the mighty, and he who rules his spirit, than he who captures the city (Proverbs 16:32).

Do you comply with employment laws but harbor discrimination in your heart?

Scripture: He will surely reprove you, if you secretly show partiality (Job 13:10).

Today's Thought: We all grow up with certain biases toward other people. Whether these biases are based on race, gender, social class, or some other characteristic, our preconceived notions create a distinct grid through which we view and evaluate the world.

If you are harboring prejudice in your heart, God calls you to examine your motives and repent of your sinful attitudes. The Bible clearly instructs us not to show partiality. Ask God to help you see the complete person. Always make promotion and hiring choices based on merit, not according to your personal preferences.

Always make promotion and hiring choices based on merit, not according to your personal preferences.

In today's highly competitive marketplace, you can't afford to let prejudice stand in the way of success. If you make wise choices and hire the best people for your business, without discrimination, your business will prosper.

To show partiality in judgment is not good (Proverbs 24:23).

Do you carefully fit individuals to their jobs?

Scripture: Since we have gifts that differ according to the grace given to us, let each exercise them accordingly (Romans 12:6).

Today's Thought: Job satisfaction and effectiveness begin with a good match between the specific tasks and duties of a job and a person's natural aptitudes, interests, and abilities. Therefore, when you need to fill a position in your company, start by developing a complete and well-conceived job description. Describe not only the duties of the job but also the work environment and kinds of interactions the employee will have on a regular basis.

Next, identify the basic skills and competencies needed to be successful in the job, as well as attributes that would identify a superior candidate for the position. With this key information at hand, you will be able to interview more effectively, focusing on the specific job requirements. Then carefully match the right individual with the job, just as you would choose the proper tool for a task.

Hire the best matched person you can find, and your business will run like a well-oiled machine.

If you spend the necessary time and effort to define each position and then hire the best matched person you can find, your business will run like a well-oiled machine.

It is not good for a person to be without knowledge, and he who makes haste with his feet errs (Proverbs 19:2).

59

Do you maintain a healthy respect for your boss?

Scripture: Rulers are not a cause of fear for good behavior, but for evil. Do you want to have no fear of authority? Do what is good, and you will have praise from the same (Romans 13:3).

Today's Thought: Some things in business are pretty straightforward. If you're consistently late for work and fail to follow instructions, your boss will fire you. It's that simple. But while an appropriate, healthy fear of losing your job may keep you in line, a better way to show your boss respect is by doing great work and taking on more responsibility. If your performance is exemplary, you will gain trust and receive praise.

If your performance is exemplary, you will gain trust and receive praise.

When you do your best work, there's no need to live in fear of your boss's opinion. Respect authority and you will maximize your career success.

Like the cold of snow in the time of harvest is a faithful messenger to those who send him (Proverbs 25:13).

Do you spend time at work with your staff or just with your peers?

Scripture: Be of the same mind toward one another; do not be haughty in mind, but associate with the lowly. Do not be wise in your own estimation (Romans 12:16).

Today's Thought: One of the most effective management tools you can buy is a comfortable pair of shoes. Then, get out where the action is and talk to employees at every level of the company. Show genuine interest, listen to their concerns, and encourage feedback.

> One of the most effective management tools you can buy is a comfortable pair of shoes.

If you associate only with other managers, you're missing a great opportunity to build your business. Million-dollar suggestions can come from the office, factory, warehouse, or loading dock. No position is too lowly to yield good ideas.

If you take time each week to "manage by wandering around," not only will employee morale improve, you will be surprised by the dividends it will return to your business.

Before destruction the heart of man is haughty, but humility goes before honor (Proverbs 18:12).

When you communicate with your staff, is your objective to help and instruct or to make yourself feel better?

Scripture: Let no unwholesome word proceed from your mouth, but only such a word as is good for edification according to the need of the moment, that it may give grace to those who hear (Ephesians 4:29).

Today's Thought: A common pitfall for managers when discussing important issues is the tendency to pontificate and make speeches. These windy discourses may make us feel better, but they rarely are helpful to others. In fact, hearing too much of the boss's perspective may hinder the process of finding a solution. Your subordinates may be reluctant to offer creative options that would run counter to your expressed viewpoint.

It's usually best to open your ears first, not your mouth.

When issues need to be resolved with staff members or coworkers, it's usually best to open your ears first, not your mouth. Once you have carefully identified the issue, listen to others' perspectives. When you are certain that you understand the situation from all sides, focus on the solution, not the problem. Avoid judgmental statements and personal attacks. Be objective and willing to teach. You will soon see a payoff in improved communication and better results.

The hearing ear and the seeing eye, the LORD has made both of them (Proverbs 20:12).

Do you delegate work to subordinates or try to do everything yourself?

Scripture: You will surely wear out, both yourself and these people who are with you, for the task is too heavy for you; you cannot do it alone (Exodus 18:18).

Today's Thought: One of the hardest skills to learn after being promoted into management is how to oversee and direct work instead of doing it ourselves. It should be obvious, however, that if we try to do everything, we will limit our effectiveness.

Instead of becoming too involved in production, delegate responsibility and invest your time in training your staff to do the job better. Outline your expectations and demonstrate effective techniques, then watch while the other person completes the task. Use your expertise to coach, encourage, and support. Allow enough room for others to take ownership of the process and discover their own improvements. You may learn a few lessons yourself.

Make your staff an extension of your effectiveness.

Make your staff an extension of your effectiveness. Productivity, efficiency, and results will multiply as you enable your staff to take on greater responsibility and grow in their skill and effectiveness.

A man's counsel is sweet to his friend (Proverbs 27:9).

Do you allow quick talkers off the hook?

Scripture: Shall a multitude of words go unanswered, and a talkative man be acquitted? (Job 11:2).

Today's Thought: When a staff person makes a blunder or fails to follow through, confront the issue squarely and ask for an explanation. Find out what went wrong and how the person will correct the problem in the future. Don't allow a long-winded response to obscure the facts. Insist on a truthful, direct answer.

Don't allow any wiggle room. Ask follow-up questions until you are satisfied that you've heard the straight story. Many questions require a yes or no answer. Insist on either a yes or no.

A bad result plus a good explanation doesn't equal a good outcome.

Remember, a bad result plus a good explanation doesn't equal a good outcome. Get the straight scoop every time to move your business forward.

It is by his deeds that a lad distinguishes himself if his conduct is pure and right (Proverbs 20:11).

Are you faithfully tending to your responsibilities?

Scripture: He who tends the fig tree will eat its fruit; and he who cares for his master will be honored (Proverbs 27:18).

Today's Thought: A peach tree left to itself will grow and yield some fruit, but the peaches are likely to be small and hard and sour. Producing a bumper crop of sweet, luscious fruit requires hard work and careful attention. Each tree must be watered, pruned, sprayed, and thinned. In addition, ongoing care is required to avoid leaf blight or an infestation of insects.

Your business is like a tree in that it requires continual attention to produce optimum results. Practice "management by walking around" to find out what's really going on. Talk to your staff, ask key questions, and listen to their suggestions and concerns.

> **Your business is like a tree in that it requires continual attention to produce optimum results.**

Stay in touch with your customers. Make a habit of calling clients to solicit their feedback, and take prompt action to resolve any issues or complaints.

Verify product or service quality yourself. Work to continually improve your processes, and remove obstacles that prevent your employees from working efficiently and effectively.

Daily diligence will pay big dividends, allowing your business to yield the sweet fruit of success.

Go to the ant, O sluggard, observe her ways and be wise (Proverbs 6:6).

Do you maintain your business focus each day, or do you drift into tasks that are fun but not essential?

Scripture: He who tills his land will have plenty of food, but he who follows empty pursuits will have poverty in plenty (Proverbs 28:19).

Today's Thought: Managing a business is a lot like farming. There isn't much that the farmer or the manager can do to directly produce results; instead, their most important responsibility is to create the proper conditions for maximum results. It's the unrewarded daily tasks—like weeding, watering, and watching the weather—that result in a bountiful harvest. Successful business management requires a lot of daily work, but the harvest makes it all worthwhile.

Maintaining a well-run organization is a top business priority. Maintaining a well-run organization is a top business priority. Identify issues that must be resolved to ensure the proper conditions for growth. Empower your employees and remove obstacles to their success. Create an environment that fosters productivity.

Do you want higher quality? Clean the restrooms. There's no better indicator of your attitude on quality than bathroom cleanliness. Identify other important "environmental" concerns and attend to them faithfully. Keep your focus on creating the proper conditions for growth, and you will reap a bounty of business success.

A faithful man will abound with blessings, but he who makes haste to be rich will not go unpunished (Proverbs 28:20).

Are you regularly improving your work skills?

Scripture: Do you see a man skilled in his work? He will stand before kings; He will not stand before obscure men (Proverbs 22:29).

Today's Thought: If you want to increase your value to your company and become a candidate for promotion, you must work continually to improve your performance and enhance your skills. The most successful people in business are lifelong learners.

Lifelong learners attend seminars to upgrade their training, take classes at the local college to broaden their understanding, and read business-related magazines and books to learn from the wisdom of others. In short, they look for every possible way to increase their knowledge, skill, and experience.

> Desiring to improve is a great strength, and your boss will be happy to encourage your efforts.

Make no excuse for not improving your work. Identify the three weakest areas of your job performance and develop a plan to address each one. Ask your boss for suggestions and support. Don't be afraid of appearing weak. Desiring to improve is a great strength, and your boss will be happy to encourage your efforts.

As you diligently work to improve, your efficiency and effectiveness will increase and your value to the company will grow.

The beginning of wisdom is: Acquire wisdom; and with all your acquiring, get understanding (Proverbs 4:7).

Are you maintaining your facilities, or is your business in a gradual decline?

Scripture: I passed by the field of the sluggard, and by the vineyard of the man lacking sense; and behold, it was completely overgrown with thistles, its surface was covered with nettles, and its stone wall was broken down (Proverbs 24:30–31).

Today's Thought: A farmer's field doesn't fall into disarray overnight, and neither does a business. It takes persistent neglect to bring about "sudden" ruin. If you're not careful, your facility and your business can go downhill one day at a time.

Make maintenance a priority, and set aside budget dollars to get the job done.

Take a good look at your building, office, and equipment. Ask managers and employees to help identify any areas that are not up to standard, or that require additional attention. Make maintenance a priority, and set aside budget dollars to get needed repairs done. Create a list of regular maintenance and improvement projects, establish a schedule, and follow through with implementation. Diligent effort and steady progress will prevent a gradual decline.

Don't let your business become overgrown with thistles. Regular attention to maintenance will keep everything running smoothly, improve employee morale, and enhance both productivity and profits.

A little sleep, a little slumber, a little folding of hands to rest—and your poverty will come in like a vagabond (Proverbs 6:10–11).

Are you placing too much trust in the integrity of your staff?

Scripture: Now he said this, not because he was concerned about the poor, but because he was a thief, and as he had the money box, he used to pilfer what was put into it (John 12:6).

Today's Thought: Employee theft is one of the major causes of business failure. Still, many owners and managers fail to audit their employees' activities. Either they don't want to put forth the effort to develop a system of checks and balances or they're afraid they will offend someone by appearing to question their integrity.

We don't want to regard others with suspicion, but keep in mind that most individuals who steal from their companies are trusted right up to the moment they are caught. In other words, you can't be too careful.

> **Most individuals who steal from their companies are trusted right up to the moment they are caught.**

The best way to ensure the financial integrity of your business without offending anyone is to establish consistent review procedures at every level. Be diligent, thorough, and fair. Remind employees that these systems are in place to protect them as well as the company.

Put the proper safeguards in place and you will avoid allowing your business to be stolen from you.

Like a bad tooth and an unsteady foot is confidence in a faithless man in time of trouble (Proverbs 25:19).

Do you have any employees reporting to two bosses?

Scripture: No one can serve two masters; for either he will hate the one and love the other, or he will hold to one and despise the other (Matthew 6:24).

Today's Thought: In this era of downsizing and cost cutting, it's not uncommon for an employee to end up "splitting time" and reporting to two managers. Unfortunately, this practice rarely works. Either the staff person becomes frustrated trying to serve two bosses or conflicts arise between the "competing" managers over assignments and expectations.

If you have any dual reporting relationships, decide which manager should be the primary supervisor.

Review your organizational structure. If you have any dual reporting relationships, decide which manager should be the primary supervisor. Establish clear and consistent guidelines for how other managers will route work to the subordinate staff person. Keep the plan simple, but complete.

The manager who loses supervisory control may not like the new arrangement at first, but ultimately frustration will be reduced for everyone.

The mind of the prudent acquires knowledge, and the ear of the wise seeks knowledge (Proverbs 18:15).

When you see a problem in your company, do you speak up or just watch things happen?

Scripture: If the watchman sees the sword coming and does not blow the trumpet, and the people are not warned, and a sword comes and takes a person from them . . . his blood I will require from the watchman's hand (Ezekiel 33:6).

Today's Thought: If you see a problem in your company, notify your supervisor. Don't be afraid to speak up. You are responsible to speak the truth, even if the situation might be uncomfortable. From that point, your boss has the responsibility to act on the information.

You are responsible to speak the truth, even if the situation might be uncomfortable.

When we fail to act promptly regarding potential problems, we become responsible for the consequences. If you point out danger signs as soon as you see them, your boss will be grateful for your concern and your contribution to the business. Your willingness to act will strengthen the company and ultimately increase your job security.

He who speaks truth tells what is right (Proverbs 12:17).

As Christians, do we forgive and forget when an employee fails to follow directions?

Scripture: He who conceals his transgressions will not prosper, but he who confesses and forsakes them will find compassion (Proverbs 28:13).

Today's Thought: As Christians we need to do as Jesus did, and look on the heart. When a staff member violates a policy or ignores instructions, he or she needs to be confronted right away with the transgression. A full and complete confession must be forthcoming, along with a demonstrated change of attitude and behavior. If behavior fails to change, then the employee must be asked to leave.

If behavior fails to change, then the employee must be asked to leave.

A staff must be willing to submit to the appropriate authority or discipline and order will break down. True confession is always followed by change. Only a change in behavior will reveal the heart.

Focus on this requirement, and your discernment will increase.

He who tends the fig tree will eat its fruit; and he who cares for his master will be honored (Proverbs 27:18).

Do you listen to your employees' suggestions, or does every idea have to be yours?

Scripture: Without consultation, plans are frustrated, but with many counselors they succeed (Proverbs 15:22).

Today's Thought: Often we ask our staff for ideas and feedback about business operations, but we don't really listen to their answers. By failing to hear others, we may miss many valuable suggestions. Consider using a suggestion system and granting both cash and noncash rewards for practical ideas you are able to implement.

Asking is only part of the process. It is important to create a receptive environment that encourages candid, honest responses. Don't rebuke someone for a critical or challenging comment. Be thankful employees are willing to speak up, and allow them to fully express their viewpoint without risk of censure.

Create a receptive environment that encourages candid, honest responses.

Don't overlook quiet employees. Ask them for feedback, draw them out, and wait for their answers. An open and honest feedback process will provide your business with the benefit of wise counsel and will enhance your business decisions.

Listen to counsel and accept discipline, that you may be wise the rest of your days (Proverbs 19:20).

In your business, do you cast off diamonds-in-the-rough as unprofitable?

Scripture: I appeal to you for . . . Onesimus, who formerly was useless to you, but now is useful both to you and to me (Philemon vv. 10–11).

Today's Thought: When Paul wrote to Philemon on behalf of the slave Onesimus, whom he was returning to his lawful place, he suggests that this formerly "useless" young man had been transformed into a valuable asset by his conversion to the truth.

Before you release an employee for unsatisfactory performance, take a good look at yourself first.

Before you release an employee for unsatisfactory performance, take a good look at yourself first. Did you give proper training for the job? Were your expectations clear and were the necessary resources available for the job to be done well? Did you give constructive feedback when improvements were needed?

Make every effort to "cut and polish" a diamond-in-the-rough before you terminate his or her employment. In doing so, you may uncover a valuable human resource for your business.

My son, do not forget my teaching, but let your heart keep my commandments (Proverbs 3:1).

Have you ever rushed to judgment and made a poor business decision?

Scripture: He who gives an answer before he hears, it is folly and shame to him (Proverbs 18:13).

Today's Thought: Often, as managers, we listen to only part of the story before we're ready to jump to conclusions. Once we've heard enough to reinforce our perception of the situation, we're ready for decisive action. The Bible calls such hastiness folly. The wise manager, on the other hand, hears all sides before passing judgment.

The wise manager hears all sides before passing judgment.

Take time to listen to all viewpoints before making important business decisions. Don't squelch employee initiative and creativity—and risk missing the best ideas and input—by being too quick to speak or act.

In hearing and considering everyone's perspective, not only will you have shown faith in the members of your team, you will also be able to make a more complete, informed decision for your business.

Do you see a man who is hasty in his words? There is more hope for a fool than for him (Proverbs 29:20).

When a coworker displays inappropriate anger, do you let him off the hook in the interest of Christian charity?

Scripture: A man of great anger shall bear the penalty, for if you rescue him, you will only have to do it again (Proverbs 19:19).

Today's Thought: Don't tolerate uncontrolled outbursts in the interest of "keeping the peace." If a staff member explodes in anger, allow him or her to bear the consequences.

Calmly convey that temper tantrums are unacceptable and insist on respectful communication at all times to you, peers, and customers. If the situation requires an apology, ask for one.

Don't tolerate uncontrolled outbursts in the interest of "keeping the peace."

Allow the offender to feel uncomfortable and ashamed. If the behavior is repeated, make it clear that any further incidents will generate significant consequences. State clearly what those consequences will be. Refuse to let an angry person off the hook and in time he or she will learn to exhibit more self-control—and you will have created a better business atmosphere.

Keeping away from strife is an honor for a man, but any fool will quarrel (Proverbs 20:3).

Do you make assumptions about your coworkers' abilities?

Scripture: Through presumption comes nothing but strife, but with those who receive counsel is wisdom (Proverbs 13:10).

Today's Thought: Sometimes we assume that our employees know exactly what we want accomplished and how we want it done, and we become frustrated if they don't produce the results we expect. However, what may be obvious to us is often unclear to others, especially if they lack our level of business experience.

Take the responsibility upon yourself to communicate your expectations clearly and completely. Outline tasks thoroughly, establish reasonable deadlines, and make sure that person to whom the task is assigned has the necessary skills and experience to do the job. Write out instructions for more complicated tasks, and ask for feedback to ensure that everything is understood.

> **Take the responsibility upon yourself to communicate your expectations clearly and completely.**

In following these guidelines not only will you experience less conflict, your staff will make fewer mistakes.

Turn to my reproof, behold, I will pour out my spirit on you; I will make my words known to you (Proverbs 1:23).

Have you ever made a mistake on a customer's order because of a faulty assumption?

Scripture: Through presumption comes nothing but strife, but with those who receive counsel is wisdom (Proverbs 13:10).

Today's Thought: When we receive orders from our customers we can easily shortcut the process, making assumptions about what they want, need, or expect—especially if it's repeat business.

Safeguard yourself and your company by developing a consistent procedure for asking questions. Make sure you understand your customer's requirements and preferences. Repeat back any specifications and clearly establish delivery dates and payment terms.

> **Safeguard yourself and your company by developing a consistent procedure for asking questions.**

Confirm all the details and write down any special requests so you don't forget. Pass along clear and complete information to your staff. Don't just assume that they'll know what to do.

Be diligent in following these steps and you will serve your customers well, reduce errors, and improve the delivery of your products and services.

Discretion will guard you, understanding will watch over you (Proverbs 2:11).

Have you ever gotten into trouble because you misunderstood your boss's instructions and were afraid to ask questions?

Scripture: Through presumption comes nothing but strife, but with those who receive counsel is wisdom (Proverbs 13:10).

Today's Thought: When we are given instructions, we are responsible for making sure we understand. If we fail to fully comprehend our boss's expectations and directions—or if we're afraid or too proud to ask for clarification—we set ourselves up to fail. Asking questions doesn't make you look bad, but failing to properly complete an assignment will.

> When our boss gives us instructions, we are responsible for making sure we understand.

Follow these simple steps to make sure you've got the whole picture: (1) Listen carefully to your manager's instructions, (2) repeat back your understanding of the requirements, and (3) clarify any points that are not clear.

Getting the facts straight from the beginning will prevent a costly error down the road and enhance your business career.

Hear my son, your father's instruction, and do not forsake your mother's teaching (Proverbs 1:8).

Do the mistakes you make at work seem to come back to haunt you?

Scripture: The deeds of a man's hands will return to him (Proverbs 12:14).

Today's Thought: The next time you are tempted to rush a job just to get the work off your desk, or the customer off the phone, or to satisfy your boss's current demands, remember that the truth of Proverbs 12:14 cuts both ways. Whether we do excellent or shoddy work, the deeds of our hands will return to us.

If you believe that you don't have time to focus on each piece of work, if you are driven to make assumptions, or if you fail to check the accuracy of your work, you will eventually find yourself reworking the job to make it right. Studies have consistently demonstrated that repairing shoddy work is more time consuming and costly than building quality into the process up front.

If you have time to do the job over, you have time to do it right the first time.

If you have time to do the job over, you have time to do it right the first time. Let only quality work pass through your hands.

He who digs a pit will fall into it, and he who rolls a stone, it will come back on him (Proverbs 26:27).

Do circumstances in your business ever cause you to panic?

Scripture: But you, keep your head in all situations (2 Timothy 4:5 NIV).

Today's Thought: Calamities in business, such as losing a major customer, may make it seem as though the sky is falling. Panic may be a natural reaction, but it never helps the situation and often makes things worse.

When circumstances take a turn for the worse, sit down, take a few deep breaths, and begin to calmly assess the situation. Identify the problem and the damage caused, and then focus on what you can do.

Panic may be a natural reaction, but it never helps the situation and often makes things worse.

If it's an issue of losing a key customer, call the customer and find out what precipitated their decision to leave. Listen carefully and make sure you understand the issues.

Next, determine whether you can take any positive action to retain the customer. Ask if any changes on your part will reverse the customer's decision. Either way, learn from your mistakes and change any business practices necessary so that other customers will stay.

Trust in the LORD with all your heart, and do not lean on your own understanding (Proverbs 3:5).

Do you plan your business activities in advance, or simply trust that everything will work out?

Scripture: The plans of the diligent lead surely to advantage, but everyone who is hasty comes surely to poverty (Proverbs 21:5).

Today's Thought: When we fail to plan, our business soon becomes unfocused because we are unclear where we want and need to go. In the midst of changing circumstances and a highly competitive marketplace, we may become confused about how we should be investing our time and resources. Confusion can quickly give way to discouragement and loss of hope when matters take a turn for the worse.

When we fail to plan, our business soon becomes unfocused.

Write a business plan. Create a vision of what the business should look like in several years and identify clear objectives, both short- and long-term. When establishing objectives, be sure that each is quantifiable and measurable. Then devise action plans to make your vision a reality.

As plans take shape and you move forward, you and your team will once again see the future with hope and enthusiasm.

Commit your works to the LORD, and your plans will be established (Proverbs 16:3).

Do you know where your business is going in the future?

Scripture: For which one of you, when he wants to build a tower, does not first sit down and calculate the cost, to see if he has enough to complete it? (Luke 14:28).

Today's Thought: Planning in business is an ongoing process. Although it's great to have five-year and ten-year plans to guide the overall direction of your company, unless you translate your plans down to daily, weekly, and monthly goals, you'll have a hard time achieving your long-term objectives.

Generally, there are three to four items that, if accomplished, would mean a 25 to 50 percent improvement in your business or department. Take at least a half-day each month, which is about 2 percent of a normal schedule, to plan the key tasks you want to accomplish for the next thirty days. Write down action steps needed to complete each task.

> Unless you translate your plans down to daily, weekly, and monthly goals, you'll have a hard time achieving your long-term objectives.

You will find that a 2 percent investment of your time will pay 1000 percent dividends in your business.

The mind of man plans his way, but the LORD directs his steps (Proverbs 16:9).

Do you spend time speculating on your business without having good information from which to work?

Scripture: But refuse foolish and ignorant speculations, knowing that they produce quarrels (2 Timothy 2:23).

Today's Thought: Some people spend countless hours and untold energy debating business issues without the benefit of knowing all the facts. The result is confusion, wasted effort, and fruitless argument based solely on conjecture and opinion.

A wise manager will gather all the facts before making business decisions.

A wise manager will gather all the facts before making business decisions. Research takes time and attention, but it results in more efficient meetings and conversations. If during a meeting, more information is needed to reach the best conclusion, adjourn the meeting for a few minutes or a few days, depending on the missing links. Then reconvene with the facts and make those decisions.

If you base your discussions on good information and work together to arrive at solutions, your energy, and that of your colleagues, will ultimately be focused on creating business success.

The lips of the wise spread knowledge, but the hearts of fools are not so (Proverbs 15:7).

Are you thorough in completing your tasks?

Scripture: His winnowing fork is in His hand, and He will thoroughly clean His threshing floor; and He will gather His wheat into the barn (Matthew 3:12).

Today's Thought: When harvesting wheat, the job is not complete until the grain is in the barn and the threshing floor is clean. Only then can the farmer take satisfaction in a job well done. In your job, do you stay at the task until the last detail is completed, or do you leave a lot of loose ends?

> The job is not complete until the grain is in the barn and the threshing floor is clean.

When attending or conducting meetings, make sure that every item for discussion results in an action plan. Take good notes, recording any items that require follow-through. Write down due dates and list who is responsible for each task. Then, incorporate necessary action items into your work schedule and get the job done. If your work is always thorough, your performance will stand out every time.

He also who is slack in his work is brother to him who destroys (Proverbs 18:9).

Are you continually striving to improve your performance, knowledge base, and professional growth?

Scripture: Be diligent to present yourself approved to God as a workman who does not need to be ashamed (2 Timothy 2:15).

Today's Thought: Effective managers and executives accept no excuse for not continually improving their job performance. Managers who fail to learn and grow will eventually be passed by.

It takes repeated sharpening to keep the edge of the sword ready for battle.

Commit yourself to reading a personal growth or business book every three months. Subscribe to and read at least one trade magazine and one general business magazine each month. Attend one or more seminars each year designed to update you in your business field. Expose yourself to new ideas and different viewpoints.

You may think you don't have time, but you can't afford not to make time for activities that will help you grow professionally. Failure to stay current will allow competitors to gain the upper hand and make inroads with your customers. It takes repeated sharpening to keep the edge of the sword ready for battle.

How blessed is the man who finds wisdom, and the man who gains understanding. For its profit is better than the profit of silver, and its gain than fine gold (Proverbs 3:13–14).

Are you a good listener?

Scripture: Concerning him we have much to say, and it is hard to explain, since you have become dull of hearing (Hebrews 5:11).

Today's Thought: If you want to be more effective on the job, sharpen your listening skills. All it takes is self-discipline and a genuine desire to hear what the other person has to say.

Start by removing all distractions. Put down the papers on your desk, establish good eye contact, and tune in. Sit still—don't wander around or answer a ringing phone or respond to E-mail. Focus on what the other person is saying, not on your next response.

If you were distracted at the beginning of the conversation, stop and ask the person to repeat what you missed. Listen actively, repeating back what you've heard, to ensure full understanding.

Eighty percent of effective communication is good listening, not talking.

Eighty percent of effective communication is good listening, not talking. Listen well, and you will do a better job and serve your customers more effectively.

Hear, my son, and accept my sayings, and the years of your life will be many (Proverbs 4:10).

87

Do you admit your mistakes to your customers, or try to hide the dirt under the rug?

Scripture: Confess your sins to one other (James 5:16).

Today's Thought: When we fall short of the mark, we must honestly confess to our customers. If we try to sweep our mistakes under the rug, eventually we'll trip over the lump and make matters worse. Most people are willing to forgive an honest mistake, but dishonesty and excuses are reasons why customers leave.

When you confess a mistake, start with an apology, not an excuse.

When you confess a mistake, start with an apology, not an excuse. Next, ask the customer how you can make amends, whether by refund, replacement, or a price adjustment. Never ask your customer to bear the consequences of your mistake.

Further, determine what changes you will make to avoid the problem in the future. Share that commitment with your customer. Then follow through and implement those changes.

Confessing shortcomings and accepting full responsibility without making excuses will keep customers coming back, and your business will stay healthy.

He who conceals his transgressions will not prosper, but he who confesses and forsakes them will find compassion (Proverbs 28:13).

Do you ever sit back and relax when business is slow, then struggle to keep up during peak times?

Scripture: The sluggard does not plow after the autumn, so he begs during the harvest and has nothing (Proverbs 20:4).

Today's Thought: Autumn plowing is an important part of farming. It prepares the soil for the next growing season, even though the crop will not be planted until spring. Despite its importance, however, some consider it an extra step after the harvest that can be overlooked.

When activity slows at work, avoid the temptation to take it easy. Look for tasks that will prepare your business for the next busy season. Clean up office and work areas, reorganize storerooms, and restock inventory.

> **When activity slows at work, avoid the temptation to take it easy.**

When traveling on business, catch up on reading, make phone calls from the airport, and keep your E-mail current.

Prepare your business for success when things are slow, and you will reap a bountiful harvest in the proper season.

Go to the ant, O sluggard, observe her ways and be wise, which, having no chief, officer or ruler, prepares her food in the summer, and gathers her provision in the harvest (Proverbs 6:6–8).

In business discussions, do you speak first or listen?

Scripture: But let everyone be quick to hear, slow to speak and slow to anger (James 1:19).

Today's Thought: During business meetings, don't be too quick to speak. Allow the leader to establish the ground rules and give others a chance to express their viewpoints. Use this time to take notes and refine the points you want to make later.

Focus on building a logical argument that covers both the pros and cons of the subject. Jot down a short outline or notes to keep organized. Then, when you're fully prepared, jump into the discussion. Confidently cover your points, supporting your position with necessary information.

Focus on building a logical argument that covers both the pros and cons of the subject.

If others disagree, ask them to explain their reasons. Listen to their input and consider your response before you reply. Again, take notes. If you believe their objections are invalid, return the discussion to the facts that support your position. If you are wrong, graciously concede.

Follow these rules and your value in meetings will increase.

Listen, for I shall speak noble things; and the opening of my lips will produce right things (Proverbs 8:6).

Do you have a mentor to help you become a more effective manager?

Scripture: And Jesus kept increasing in wisdom and stature, and in favor with God and men (Luke 2:52).

Today's Thought: One method for improving your effectiveness in business is to find a mentor. A mentor is someone with more business and life experience than you who can coach you and give you advice. You may find a mentor within your company, but it isn't necessary. In fact, a mentor who works somewhere else will provide a valuable measure of objectivity.

To find a mentor, look for a person with three key qualifications: spiritual maturity, extensive business experience, and a similar temperament to yours. Your mentor should also be the same sex to avoid any issues of impropriety.

Establish an open and honest relationship with your mentor; then pay attention and grow in wisdom.

When approaching possible mentors, explain that you want to learn from their experience and benefit from their insight. Ask if they would be willing to meet with you face-to-face once a month for an hour. Establish an open and honest relationship with your mentor; then pay attention and grow in wisdom.

Commit to revisiting the obligation in one year. Some mentoring relationships may last a season, others, a lifetime.

For if you cry for discernment, lift your voice for understanding (Proverbs 2:3).

How do you maintain business leadership?

Scripture: Loyalty and truth preserve the king, and he upholds his throne by righteousness (Proverbs 20:28).

Today's Thought: The legitimacy of your leadership is established and preserved when you demonstrate loyalty to customers and colleagues alike, and when you conduct business according to principles of righteousness.

If you create a pleasant and supportive work environment, offer appropriate encouragement, and fairly compensate employees, you will encourage your staff to serve you and your company faithfully.

The legitimacy of your leadership is established and preserved when you demonstrate loyalty to customers and colleagues.

If you demonstrate your commitment to customers by serving them without fail, by pricing your products fairly, and by continuously striving to improve your service, they will keep coming back for more—and they'll tell their friends!

Loyalty is a two-way street. As you build faith with others through consistency and fairness, they will remain loyal to you and support your leadership—and your business will continue to grow and prosper.

Many a man proclaims his own loyalty, but who can find a trustworthy man? A righteous man who walks in his integrity—how blessed are his sons after him (Proverbs 20:6–7).

Are you willing to stand behind your products and services, even if it costs you money?

Scripture: My eyes shall be upon the faithful of the land, that they may dwell with me; He who walks in a blameless way is the one who will minister to me (Psalm 101:6).

Today's Thought: A key element of integrity is standing behind your products and services. Does your return policy favor the customer or your business? Do you seek to satisfy your customer, or do you quibble over the fine print?

When you receive complaints—and everyone does at some point—do you become defensive or do you listen to your customer and work out a reasonable solution? I once heard a business owner proudly crow that he saves thousands of dollars by holding to a thirty-day policy for defects, not one day more.

A key element of integrity is standing behind your products and services.

If you have to make a mistake, err on the side of the customer. Work out a generous solution that allows your customer to go home happy. If someone is dissatisfied, take the product back. You may forgo profits in the short run, but you will gain invaluable customer loyalty, and your long-term success will be assured.

A faithful man will abound with blessings, but he who makes haste to be rich will not go unpunished (Proverbs 28:20).

When a staff member bends your ear on an issue do you take immediate action or decide to dig deeper?

Scripture: A single witness shall not rise up against a man on account of any iniquity or any sin which he has committed; on the evidence of two or three witnesses a matter shall be confirmed (Deuteronomy 19:15).

Today's Thought: In court cases, witnesses are cross-examined to determine the full truth about a situation, and as many witnesses are called as have pertinent information. When a staff member brings an issue to your attention, you may need to employ the same processes before taking action. Ask questions; dig a little deeper. Bring in any others who could add more information on the subject. Often a perspective will look valid until examined from another viewpoint.

When a staff member brings an issue to your attention ... dig a little deeper.

Establish a habit of thorough investigation to determine the reality behind an individual's point of view, and don't take action without gathering all the facts. Due diligence will result in wise and profitable decisions that will keep your business on track.

The first to plead his case seems just, until another comes and examines him (Proverbs 18:17).

Do you provide the highest quality product or service?

Scripture: Whatever your hand finds to do, verily, do it with all your might (Ecclesiastes 9:10).

Today's Thought: In the rush to keep the production line moving or to ship products on time, do you ever overlook inferior quality? As we strive to keep our businesses cost-competitive, we might be tempted to cut corners or look for shortcuts on quality. Don't fall into that trap. Instead, develop a standard to ensure the highest quality in all your products.

Instill in your employees a sense of pride in your company's products and services. Insist on superior quality every time, and hold your staff accountable. Watch the quality even when your customer may not notice the effect immediately.

Insist on superior quality every time, and hold your staff accountable.

Consider installing a large sign in your shipping department that reads, "If you aren't proud of every product, don't ship it." Then allow your team members to stop any product before delivery if the quality is not up to standard. If you build a reputation for consistent quality, customers will flock to you.

Differing weights and differing measures, both of them are abominable to the LORD (Proverbs 20:10).

Do you desire to earn a promotion?

Scripture: The hand of the diligent will rule, but the slack hand will be put to forced labor (Proverbs 12:24).

Today's Thought: Many workers wish for a promotion, but the one who is willing to earn it usually comes out on top.

Identify a position to which you would like to be promoted. Make your interest known to your boss and ask what criteria will be used for selection. Then buckle down and work diligently toward accomplishing your purpose.

Don't neglect your present duties. Faithfully carry out the responsibilities of your current position while preparing yourself for the next step. Ask your boss to suggest areas for improvement and respond quickly to shore up areas of weakness. Pursue additional training or enroll in classes that will help you to be better prepared. Any advancement will come with some price, so determine the cost and commit to the work needed to achieve that next step.

Faithfully carry out the responsibilities of your current position while preparing yourself for the next step.

As you demonstrate diligence and effective performance, your boss will consider you for promotion and entrust you with additional authority.

Poor is he who works with a negligent hand, but the hand of the diligent makes rich (Proverbs 10:4).

How do you deal with unproductive employees in your business?

Scripture: Every branch in Me that does not bear fruit, He takes away; and every branch that bears fruit, He prunes it, that it may bear more fruit (John 15:2).

Today's Thought: We have a responsibility to establish clear standards for the quality and quantity of work we expect from our staff. If an individual's work is not up to par, we must seek to correct the deficiency.

If an individual's work is not up to par, seek to correct the deficiency.

Start by monitoring job performance, praising good work, and identifying areas of weakness. If someone's performance is unacceptable, explain the improvements that are needed. If poor quality work continues, issue a written warning, detailing what must be corrected. Ask the employee how you can help them to improve.

If the problem still persists, dismiss the employee. Chances are that the person is not well suited for the job and would continue to struggle no matter what. Focus on building productivity and your business will bear fruit.

Why is there a price in the hand of a fool to buy wisdom, when he has no sense? (Proverbs 17:16).

Do you encourage your boss at work?

Scripture: But Moses' hands were heavy. Then they took a stone and put it under him, and he sat on it; and Aaron and Hur supported his hands, one on one side and one on the other. Thus his hands were steady until the sun set (Exodus 17:12).

Today's Thought: The cliché that it's lonely at the top is true. As the burden of responsibility increases, it's easy for a manager to feel isolated and discouraged. Your boss needs your encouragement and moral support.

When your boss does something that you appreciate, speak up.

When your boss does something you appreciate, speak up. Let him know how his actions have helped you. Praise examples of his good leadership.

Look for and ask your boss how you can help him in his responsibilities. As you help hold up his hands, success for all will follow.

Encouragement and enthusiasm are contagious. If you take it upon yourself to praise your boss's efforts, you will encourage him to provide more positive leadership. Better leadership will, in turn, result in greater success for the business, which benefits everyone.

A friend loves at all times, and a brother is born for adversity (Proverbs 17:17).

Are you able to recover from a failure in your job or business?

Scripture: Though he fall, he shall not be utterly cast down; for the LORD upholds him with His hand (Psalm 37:24 NKJV).

Today's Thought: Hardship and challenges test our faith and make us stronger. The same principle applies on the job. If you've suffered a failure in your business, stop for a moment to evaluate what went wrong. Decide whether you need to adjust your plan or change course completely, then get back on track.

Effective managers often learn more from their failures and disappointments than from their successes. When things go wrong, identify one or two things you can learn from the experience.

> Learn from your mistakes, and don't pay twice for the same lesson.

Apply the "failure principle" when interviewing job applicants. Ask prospects to tell you about two or three mistakes they've made and what they learned from them. Look for examples in which the applicant suffered a defeat but learned a great lesson.

The bottom line in overcoming adversity is this: Learn from your mistakes, and don't pay twice for the same lesson.

Incline your ear and hear the words of the wise, and apply your mind to my knowledge (Proverbs 22:17).

Do you carefully research the competition?

Scripture: Send out for yourself men so that they may spy out the land of Canaan (Numbers 13:2).

Today's Thought: Researching the competition is one often-overlooked key to success. The more you understand your competitors, the better your chances of winning in the marketplace. However, many small- to mid-size companies simply do not expend the effort.

Avoid anything illegal or unethical, but do everything you reasonably can to check out the competition. At the very least, check out your competitors' Web sites; read their ads, brochures, and marketing materials, and become familiar with their products and services. Better yet, stop by their place of business to get a feel for how they operate and to evaluate the quality of their customer service. Place an order, if it's practical, to see how quickly they ship their products and how they treat their customers.

> **The more you understand your competitors, the better your chances of winning in the marketplace.**

When you thoroughly understand the competition, you can take decisive action to move your business ahead.

If you say, "See, we did not know this," does He not consider it who weighs the hearts? (Proverbs 24:12).

Are you faithful in everything you deliver to your customers?

Scripture: His master said to him, "Well done, good and faithful slave; you were faithful with a few things, I will put you in charge of many things, enter into the joy of your master" (Matthew 25:21).

Today's Thought: A bank's computer specialist was bragging about keeping the bank's ATM machines working 98.5 percent of the time. The bank president responded, "You mean to say that our customers can't get their money out of our bank two-and-a-half hours per week—and you're happy?"

Faithfulness in the little things will eventually show itself in the big things. Attention to detail results in better quality, and quality always sells. A commitment to continued improvement, rather than contentment, will result in a company culture of upgrading customer service.

Don't settle for less than exceeding your customers' expectations.

Timex has built its reputation on the promise that their product "takes a licking and keeps on ticking." If you build that kind of quality into your product or service, your customers will keep coming back for more. Don't settle for less than exceeding your customers' expectations.

Wealth gained by dishonesty will be diminished, but he who gathers by labor will increase (Proverbs 13:11 NKJV)

Do you struggle with tough decisions at work?

Scripture: How can I alone bear the load and burden of you and your strife? (Deuteronomy 1:12).

Today's Thought: Accept responsibility for the decisions you can make, and make them. Don't push decisions up to your boss that have been delegated to you and that you are capable of making. Make a habit of solving problems, not creating new ones.

But when you are stumped by a decision at work and need help, don't let pride stop you from asking your boss **Don't let pride stop you from asking your boss for assistance.** for assistance. There's no point in struggling if your boss's experience and insight can help to resolve the issue more quickly. The key is to know when to ask for help.

When you approach your boss for help, outline the issues, give your perspective, and then ask for advice and counsel. Most managers are willing, even eager, to assist in making decisions, especially when you have done your homework.

Learn from your boss's example, and your own decision-making skills will improve.

For wisdom will enter your heart, and knowledge will be pleasant to your soul (Proverbs 2:10).

Have you stayed too long in your comfort zone?

Scripture: So Joshua said to the sons of Israel, "How long will you put off entering to take possession of the land which the LORD, the God of your fathers, has given you?" (Joshua 18:3).

Today's Thought: As the years go by in our business, we reach plateaus where life is comfortable and the work is manageable but not challenging. At times like these, we need to set our sights on the next opportunity and take action.

Get out of your office and work to secure a new customer. Roll out the new product line you have been pondering for months, or follow through on a new innovation you have considered. Today we live in a fast-moving world, and maintaining your position is rarely an option. Either move forward or be prepared to be pushed back.

Either move forward or be prepared to be pushed back.

Success is waiting for you to take the bull by the horns—but it won't wait long. Know when to move forward in your business to create opportunities, generate continued growth, and enhance your progress.

A little sleep, a little slumber, a little folding of the hands to rest, then your poverty will come as a robber, and your want like an armed man (Proverbs 24:33–34).

Do you relay instructions and directives to your staff clearly and completely?

Scripture: You shall not add to the word which I am commanding you, nor take away from it, that you may keep the commandments of the LORD your God which I command you (Deuteronomy 4:2).

Today's Thought: At times, we may want to soften a directive that comes down from senior management to protect staff from what we believe are harsh words. We use the bluntness of the message as an excuse for not dealing honestly with the issue.

The best approach is always to be direct and honest.

Unfortunately, when we mince words, we often make the situation worse instead of helping. If management has said that the plant will close unless efficiency is increased 20 percent, there's no way to sugarcoat the truth.

Failing to explain the entire message is also a form of dishonesty. Just as you expect subordinates to pass on your messages, you must pass on those from your boss.

The best approach is always to be direct and honest. That way everyone knows the score and each team member can pitch in to help reach the required goal. Knowledge is power, and sharing knowledge empowers your employees, even when the truth is hard to hear.

Better is open rebuke than love that is concealed (Proverbs 27:5).

Do you give a full day's effort at work?

Scripture: Give and it will be given to you; good measure, pressed down, shaken together, running over, they will pour into your lap. For whatever measure you deal out to others, it will be dealt to you in return (Luke 6:38).

Today's Thought: A staff member once complained to me about going home tired most days. Though I think he was looking for some sympathy, what I gave him was encouragement to keep giving his all at work. At times, if we allow ourselves to become overly sympathetic rather than focusing on the work at hand, we are not providing the best leadership.

There's nothing wrong with being tired at the end of the day.

While I would agree that we should not be dragging ourselves home at night unable to function after a day at work, there's nothing wrong with being tired at the end of the day. If we want to reap the highest rewards from our work, we must be willing to expend enough of ourselves to be tired.

Put your full energy and effort on the line each day, and success will follow.

The soul of the sluggard craves and gets nothing, but the soul of the diligent is made fat (Proverbs 13:4).

Do you step out boldly, only to look back at the first sign of trouble?

Scripture: Is this not the word that we spoke to you in Egypt, saying, "Leave us alone that we may serve the Egyptians"? For it would have been better for us to serve the Egyptians than to die in the wilderness (Exodus 14:12).

Today's Thought: Launching new ventures requires a bold commitment to press on, even when the going gets rough. If you don't stay focused on your purpose, your perspective may become warped. Like the Israelites, who looked back with longing at their slavery in Egypt, you might begin to think things were better in the past. But while you are looking backward, you may miss potential blessings on the road ahead.

The challenge you don't want to face is the one to tackle first.

Often, when making a major change in business direction, morale will drop before the improvement is understood and felt by each team member. Recognize that those times will come and be prepared to lead.

Confront your fears, and refuse to settle for the old comfort zone. The challenge you don't want to face is the one to tackle first. Start there, then move on. You will be uncomfortable at first, but as you press on your confidence—and success—will follow.

The wicked flee when no one is pursuing, but the righteous are bold as a lion (Proverbs 28:1).

Do you think of great ideas, only to forget them later?

Scripture: And you shall write them on the doorposts of your house and on your gates (Deuteronomy 11:20).

Today's Thought: All ideas have value, and some may be worth a lot of money for your business. But if you can't remember your best ideas, you may miss some great opportunities. Develop the habit of writing down all new thoughts in your planner, a notebook, or on a slip of paper.

Sort your ideas by topic for easy reference and retrieval. Then create an idea file to store everything. Don't worry about the form of the file as much as creating and using the system.

> If you can't remember your best ideas, you may miss some great opportunities.

Schedule time each month to look over your ideas. Reading back through old thoughts might trigger even more ideas. Some you can use now, some will have to wait until later, and others you may discard. The important thing is that you keep track of your ideas so they don't slip away.

Bind them on your fingers; write them on the tablet of your heart (Proverbs 7:3).

Is your customer service lukewarm?

Scripture: So because you are lukewarm, and neither hot nor cold, I will spit you out of My mouth (Revelation 3:16).

Today's Thought: If you want to succeed in today's competitive marketplace, you must have a passion for serving your customers. Just going through the motions of customer service will eventually destroy your business. Don't think that the quality of your product alone will carry the day.

Imagine receiving a lukewarm latte from your neighborhood coffee house, only to be told, "Hey, that's the best I can do!" You'd find your next cup of coffee someplace else, right?

Develop a passion for serving your customers.

Make a commitment to provide only the best customer service. Ask your customers for feedback and suggestions for how you can improve, then work tirelessly to put those ideas into action. If you cannot honestly develop a passion for serving your customers, you may be in the wrong business.

Stoke the fires of customer service and make your business a red-hot success.

Better is a dish of vegetables where love is, than a fattened ox and hatred with it (Proverbs 15:17).

Do you put God first in your business life?

Scripture: Keep the words of this covenant to do them, that you may prosper in all that you do (Deuteronomy 29:9).

Today's Thought: A business conducted according to biblical principles will inevitably grow and prosper. When you apply God's Word faithfully in your business, customers will be attracted by your integrity and dependability, your attitude of service, and the quality of your products.

Employees will likewise want to be part of an organization that demonstrates vision, commitment, fairness, faithfulness, mercy, truth, and a genuine concern for their well-being.

Non-Christians may not understand the basis for your outstanding service and commitment to quality, but when they ask, be ready to show them the importance of salvation, the truth of God's Word, and its practical application to business and life.

A business conducted according to biblical principles will inevitably grow and prosper.

If you commit your business to the Lord and walk with integrity, customers will flock to your doors, your employees will remain loyal and true, and your company will grow in righteousness and favor.

Righteousness exalts a nation, but sin is a disgrace to any people (Proverbs 14:34).

Are you critical of others when you yourself have not followed through?

Scripture: You hypocrite, first take the log out of your own eye, and then you will see clearly enough to take the speck out of your brother's eye (Matthew 7:5).

Today's Thought: What kind of example are you setting for your staff? Are you showing up for work on time, honoring customer commitments, and keeping your promises to other members of the team? Or is your management style more "do as I say and not as I do"?

Is your management style more "do as I say and not as I do"?

As business leaders, when we allow ourselves to be held accountable by others, we increase our authority to hold others accountable. But if we keep one standard for ourselves and another, stricter, standard for our subordinates, we undermine our credibility and weaken employee morale.

Like it or not, our actions speak louder to staff than our commands. Effective managers build trust through integrity, consistency, and follow-through. Your leadership will be enhanced as you set a worthy example in your business.

It is by his deeds that a lad distinguishes himself if his conduct is pure and right (Proverbs 20:11).

Are you worth more than you're paid?

Scripture: I, therefore, the prisoner of the Lord, entreat you to walk in a manner worthy of the calling with which you have been called (Ephesians 4:1).

Today's Thought: A common complaint among workers is that they aren't being paid what they're worth. But have you ever done a cost/benefit analysis on yourself and your work?

First, calculate the cost of your time to your employer or business, including benefits and other perks. We often forget the cost of benefits, which often run 40 percent or more of salary. Then figure the value of the work you produce. Does your worth exceed your cost? The best way to gain and maintain job security is to be worth more than you're paid, because a business can't afford to keep someone who is paid more than he or she is worth.

> The best way to gain job security is to be worth more than you're paid.

Treat each day and hour at your job as a valuable commodity and make the most of it, because time is money. Make every day count in your business and you will enjoy maximum job security, success, and satisfaction.

The wages of the righteous is life, the income of the wicked, punishment (Proverbs 10:16).

Do you manage your time well each day at work?

Scripture: Teach us to number our days, that we may gain a heart of wisdom (Psalm 90:12 NKJV).

Today's Thought: On the job we face a flood of pressures, tasks, and responsibilities every day. If we don't manage our priorities and work on first things first, we'll end up drowning in tasks that are urgent but not necessarily important.

Before you start each day, make a list of key tasks to be accomplished. Review the list and determine if you have time to accomplish everything. Set priorities on your tasks and do the most important ones first. Stay focused, review your list throughout the day, and cross off each item when completed.

Set priorities on your tasks and do the most important ones first.

Realize that interruptions will happen, so schedule time to answer phone calls and respond to E-mail messages, but don't let those tasks steal your best time. Develop strategies for minimizing interruptions and distractions. Stick to your key tasks, and your key work will get done.

When the whirlwind passes, the wicked is no more, but the righteous has an everlasting foundation (Proverbs 10:25).

Do you encourage teamwork in your business?

Scripture: Bear one another's burdens, and thus fulfill the law of Christ (Galatians 6:2).

Today's Thought: Not long after a friend and I were seated in a busy restaurant, the manager brought water and took our order for soft drinks.

A few minutes later, a waiter delivered the drinks and took our food order. When the food was served, it was yet another server who brought the lunch hot to our table. After our meal, I commended the manager for the teamwork we had observed.

He thanked me and explained how they trained their employees to help out. "If we see a need, we step in and help. If an order is up and the waiter is unavailable, another waiter will pitch in to deliver the meal fresh."

> "If we see a need, we step in and help."

No business will succeed well without teamwork, so instill the attitude in your staff of helping each other to serve the customer. Model it yourself and insist that everyone else follow through. Reward publicly examples of excellent teamwork while consistently correcting poor team efforts. Encourage your employees in teamwork and your business will enjoy great success.

He who is generous will be blessed, for he gives some of his food to the poor (Proverbs 22:9).

Do you allow past failures to keep you from success today?

Scripture: Do not call to mind the former things, or ponder things of the past. Behold, I will do something new (Isaiah 43:18–19).

Today's Thought: Everybody fails. Those who succeed discover how to pick up the pieces of their failures and move on. Learn from your failures so that you don't repeat the same mistakes, but don't be intimidated by an occasional misstep or stumble. Keep looking ahead.

Those who succeed discover how to pick up the pieces of their failures and move on.

Establish a plan to overcome common or repeated obstacles. If you can avoid it, don't pay twice for the same experience. Work your plan out point-by-point, monitoring progress at each step.

If you learn from past mistakes, you will no longer have to look back with regret or sorrow. Today is a new day, filled with new possibilities and fresh chances. Set your mind on creating something new and you can move forward with confidence and achieve business success.

For a righteous man falls seven times, and rises again (Proverbs 24:16).

Do you fail to invest in staff training because you're watching the bottom line?

Scripture: He trains my hands for battle, so that my arms can bend a bow of bronze (Psalm 18:34).

Today's Thought: Companies that fail to train their employees list several reasons for neglecting this important priority:

- It's expensive and they don't want to invest in people who may leave for other companies.
- Managers are too busy with their own responsibilities to plan and implement effective training.
- Training pulls people away from "getting the job done."

Not training your workers can result in higher costs from turnover, mistakes, and inefficiency.

Although it's true that proper training costs money, takes time, and requires planning, not training your workers can result in higher costs from turnover, mistakes, and inefficiency.

Studies have shown that on-the-job training makes workers 10 to 35 percent more effective, it usually requires very little cash, and it may make employees more loyal and committed.

Establish a training program now. Determine your employees' needs, then develop a plan of instruction. Train well, and reap thousands of dollars in additional profits.

Take my instruction, and not silver, and knowledge rather than choicest gold (Proverbs 8:10).

115

Do you hire applicants with a yearning for learning?

Scripture: Do not reprove a scoffer, lest he hate you. Reprove a wise man, and he will love you (Proverbs 9:8).

Today's Thought: When interviewing prospective employees, ask them to give three examples of lessons they've learned from previous bosses. If they can't think of anything, consider that a red flag. Employees often don't learn because they *won't* learn.

> When interviewing prospective employees, ask them to give three examples of lessons they've learned from previous bosses.

When you find applicants who demonstrate a willingness and ability to learn on the job, ask them what they hope to learn from you and your company. If their answers reveal ambitions that are in line with your company's needs, chances are that you've found an employee who is poised for long-term growth and effectiveness on the job.

Ask the right questions to determine the right attitude before hiring, and you'll acquire the best staff for long-term growth.

Drive out the scoffer, and contention will go out, even strife and dishonor will cease (Proverbs 22:10).

Do you make your own decisions, ignoring company policy?

Scripture: He who keeps a royal command experiences no trouble, for a wise heart knows the proper time and procedure (Ecclesiastes 8:5).

Today's Thought: An employee who makes independent decisions, ignoring company policy, can be summed up in two words: loose cannon. Like sailors on the deck of a ship, managers quickly learn to avoid loose cannons or find a way to tie them down.

To be effective, anchor your decisions in company policies and procedures. Don't always assume your way is better. If you do have a suggestion for improvement, work through the proper channels to propose the idea to your boss or the owner of the company.

> Like sailors on the deck of a ship, managers quickly learn to avoid loose cannons or find a way to tie them down.

Select a time when you can approach your boss without disrupting the flow of work and ask for sufficient time to make your proposal. Outline the advantages of your plan and the expected results. Ask for feedback. Invite questions and be willing to modify your plan.

Run your better ideas through proper channels and your value as a team member will increase.

By forbearance a ruler may be persuaded (Proverbs 25:15).

Do you maintain your business property well?

Scripture: If a man is lazy, the rafters sag; if his hands are idle, the house leaks (Ecclesiastes 10:18 NIV).

Today's Thought: When we're concentrating on "getting the job done," little maintenance details will often escape us. Over time, though, these minor oversights can add up to major repairs or other problems. Don't be so focused on output that you neglect one of your most important business assets—your facility.

Commit at least one hour per month to walk around your business with a notebook. Jot down items that need maintenance or repair. Develop a plan for washing the windows, cleaning the carpets, and totally cleaning the bathrooms on a regular basis. Spruce up other parts of the building as the need arises.

> **Over time, minor oversights can add up to major repairs or other problems.**

A roof doesn't leak all at once. It usually begins with a few loose shingles, worn-out caulking, or problems with the gutters. Regular maintenance will solve these issues early and prevent bigger problems.

Keep an eye on your building, schedule regular maintenance, and make sure the work gets done. Then your rafters won't sag and your roof won't leak.

By wisdom a house is built, and by understanding it is established (Proverbs 24:3).

As a manager, do you keep promises to your staff?

Scripture: It is better that you should not vow than that you should vow and not pay (Ecclesiastes 5:5).

Today's Thought: In our efforts to motivate our employees, we may be tempted to make promises we can't necessarily keep. For example, we may dangle the carrot of a possible raise in front of our employees to try to increase productivity. But if we need our own boss's approval before adjusting someone's salary, we are setting ourselves up for a fall. Having to pull back from a promise may devastate morale and undercut our leadership.

Be careful not to make commitments outside of your authority. If your decisions require final approval from your boss, don't act like it's your call. And don't talk to your staff about promotions and raises until you have complete agreement and approval from your own superiors.

> **Be careful not to make commitments outside of your authority.**

If you only make promises you know you can keep, all will appreciate your honesty and integrity.

Discretion will guard you, understanding will watch over you (Proverbs 2:11).

Do you change suppliers every time someone cuts the price by a penny?

Scripture: So in everything, do to others what you would have them do to you (Matthew 7:12 NIV).

Today's Thought: We all want our customers to stick with us through thick and thin, but are we willing to extend the same commitment to our suppliers? Or are we ready to jump ship every time a new vendor comes along with a lower price?

Everyone likes to save money, but before you change suppliers, count the full cost. How much time will your staff spend adjusting to the new vendor? Will the supplier be as dependable in terms of quality and delivery? Will they work with you to solve problems? Are they financially stable and able to perform?

Everyone likes to save money, but before you change suppliers, count the full cost.

Long-term relationships with vendors and suppliers often yield the best results. They know your needs, and their performance and reliability has already been established. If the issue is cost, give your regular vendor an opportunity to match the price. Don't be quick to change suppliers unless the benefits significantly outweigh the costs to your business.

Do not forsake your own friend or your father's friend (Proverbs 27:10).

Are you willing to learn from your subordinates?

Scripture: In much wisdom there is much grief, and increasing knowledge results in increasing pain (Ecclesiastes 1:18).

Today's Thought: As managers who want to grow and improve, we should be willing to learn a few lessons from our subordinates. Of course, it can be be painful to hear honest feedback from the people who report to us, but they often have the clearest view of our strengths and weaknesses.

If you're willing to take the plunge, ask your staff for three recommendations on how you can improve your leadership. Make it safe for honest feedback, listen to their comments, and do not become defensive.

If you receive consistent criticism, the feedback is probably on target. Take it to the Lord, change your behavior, and strengthen your weaknesses.

As you open your mind to constructive input—even from your subordinates—your leadership will become more effective, and your team will grow stronger.

> It can be be painful to hear honest feedback from the people who report to us, but they often have the clearest view of our strengths and weaknesses.

Heed instruction and be wise, and do not neglect it (Proverbs 8:33).

Have you earned your employer's complete trust?

Scripture: Only no accounting shall be made with them for the money delivered into their hands, for they deal faithfully (2 Kings 22:7).

Today's Thought: Webster's Dictionary defines the word *faithful* as "steadfast in affection or allegiance; loyal; firm in adherence to promises or in observance of duty; conscientious." Do those words describe your performance on the job? Do you follow through every time? Are you reliable? Do you demonstrate loyalty to your boss and organization?

Proven faithfulness builds trust. And along with trust comes greater responsibility and authority.

Proven faithfulness builds trust with our employer. And along with trust comes greater responsibility and authority.

If you haven't yet proven yourself faithful, it's never too late to start doing the right thing. Start now to develop the characteristics of loyalty, steadfastness, diligence, and perseverance. Apply these standards to your daily decisions, measure each day's work against these criteria, and you will begin to establish a reputation for faithfulness.

Many a man proclaims his own loyalty, but who can find a trustworthy man? (Proverbs 20:6).

Do you run effective meetings, or does the discussion drift off in every direction?

Scripture: Therefore I run in such a way, as not without aim (1 Corinthians 9:26).

Today's Thought: We've all sat through meetings that wandered from pillar to post and accomplished little. Make the most of your meetings by staying focused and keeping the discussion on track. Before you schedule a meeting, first make sure it is really necessary. Meeting just to meet is a tremendous waste of time.

Determine key decisions or objectives to be accomplished and state them clearly. Write an agenda outlining topics to be covered and allocate time for each.

> **Make the most of your meetings by staying focused and keeping the discussion on track.**

Use the agenda to keep the group on track. If the discussion starts to wander, quickly bring it back to the point, reminding everyone of the meeting's objectives. When the necessary information has been gathered, or a decision reached, end the meeting.

You will accomplish more, and your team will become more productive, if you can make meetings as effective as they can be.

Heed instruction and be wise, and do not neglect it (Proverbs 8:33).

How do you review your employees and determine raises?

Scripture: The LORD our God will have no part in unrighteousness, or partiality (2 Chronicles 19:7).

Today's Thought: Some people are just easier to get along with. We see eye to eye, share the same interests, and have common perspectives. When some of those people are employees, it can be easy to play favorites. But when the time comes to give reviews, we must be objective and impartial.

The Bible clearly teaches that we're to avoid partiality. To remove subjectivity from our decision-making we need to set up clear, written objectives for every job. Determine in advance what results will be considered outstanding, satisfactory, or unacceptable.

> **When the time comes to give reviews, we must be objective and impartial.**

Communicate the requirements clearly to your employees, and make sure they understand. Then measure each team member using the same objective system. If your employees understand what's expected, and you keep your evaluations objective, you will end up promoting and rewarding your best team members.

If a king judges the poor with truth, his throne will be established forever (Proverbs 29:14).

Do you provide the best tools for your staff?

Scripture: Behold, I have made you a new, sharp threshing sledge with double edges (Isaiah 41:15).

Today's Thought: Few things are more frustrating on the job than having to work without the proper tools, or with equipment in need of repair. You can't provide your staff with second-rate tools and expect first-rate results. In today's marketplace "sharpening the ax" is fundamental wisdom for woodcutters and well-run businesses alike. Effective tools, whether office equipment, factory machinery, or computer software, will sharpen the productivity of your staff and allow them to operate more efficiently.

In today's marketplace, "sharpening the ax" is fundamental wisdom for woodcutters and well-run businesses alike.

Acquire the best equipment you can afford, and don't skimp just to protect today's bottom line. Better quality tends to last longer, so view your equipment expense as an investment for the long term. If you equip your staff with the tools and supplies they need to be successful, your business will grow and you will profit well beyond your investment.

The refining pot is for silver and the furnace for gold, but the LORD tests hearts (Proverbs 17:3).

Are you able to persuade your boss about a correct course of action?

Scripture: Present your case. . . . Bring forward your strong arguments (Isaiah 41:21).

Today's Thought: When you have a business initiative that requires your boss's approval, don't be shy about it. First, carefully prepare your case and then ask for a meeting. When you have your boss's attention, simply outline the facts, present your proposal, clarify the action requiring approval, and detail the expected results.

Do your homework, and back up your position with facts, not just feelings. Stick to compelling arguments and skip the weak ones. If your boss prefers to see information presented in a particular way, do it that way. Keep the discussion focused, and don't forget to ask for a decision at the end.

If your boss prefers to see information presented in a particular way, do it that way.

If you arm yourself with preparation, adapt your presentation to suit your boss's preferences, and boldly make your case, you will become more effective, and ultimately more valuable to your employer.

Through patience a ruler can be persuaded, and a gentle tongue can break a bone (Proverbs 25:15 NIV).

Have you been asked to give a personal guarantee for a business debt?

Scripture: Do not be among those who give pledges, among those who become sureties for debts. If you have nothing with which to pay, why should he take your bed from under you? (Proverbs 22:26–27).

Today's Thought: Business owners are often required to sign personal guarantees for business debt, but this should be avoided whenever possible. Personal guarantees place all assets at risk in the event of a loan default.

Never sign a personal guarantee on a business debt without your spouse's informed consent and agreement. Your house is usually included in a personal guarantee, and you could lose your home if you fail to make your payments.

Be conservative in your financing and careful about making a pledge. Keep your house as your home and not as collateral for a business loan.

> **Never sign a personal guarantee on a business debt without your spouse's informed consent and agreement.**

My son, if you have become surety for your neighbor, . . . deliver yourself like a gazelle from the hunter's hand, and like the bird from the hand of the fowler (Proverbs 6:1, 5).

Do you pad your personal salary at the expense of your employees?

Scripture: Do not merely look out for your own personal interests, but also for the interests of others (Philippians 2:4).

Today's Thought: The best business owners pay an appropriate living to their staff and keep their own compensation commensurate with their investment in the business. If the business can't afford a competitive wage for its employees, the owner shouldn't be feathering his own nest. It's okay to eat well and have a nice home, but not at the expense of your staff.

If the business can't afford a competitive wage for its employees, the owner shouldn't be feathering his own nest.

In the ancient Near East, shepherds didn't eat until the sheep were fed and didn't rest until the sheep were safe. By caring for their flocks before themselves, the shepherds protected their livelihood and the source of their supply.

If your employees know you have their best interests at heart, they become loyal. They appreciate your genuine concern and the security of working for a company that is run with integrity. Take care of your employees and your employees will take care of your business.

Better is a little with righteousness than great income with injustice (Proverbs 16:8).

Are you honoring the Lord with the proceeds of your business?

Scripture: "Bring the whole tithe into the storehouse . . . and test Me now in this," says the LORD of hosts, "if I will not open for you the windows of heaven, and pour out for you a blessing until there is no more need" (Malachi 3:10).

Today's Thought: Do you tithe from the proceeds of your business and not just from your personal salary? When you make a priority of supporting the Lord's work from the profits from your business, he promises to bless you with even greater abundance.

Furthermore, he calls you to honor him in the way you conduct your business. Keep your commitments and honor your word. Pay your bills on time and provide reasonable wages. Produce top quality products, offer superior service, and strive to exceed your customers' expectations.

> **When you make a priority of supporting the Lord's work, he promises to bless you.**

If you maintain these practices consistently, the Lord will be honored, and your business will prosper.

Honor the LORD from your wealth, and from the first of all your produce; so your barns will be filled with plenty, and your vats will overflow with new wine (Proverbs 3:9–10).

Do you value every member of your business team?

Scripture: For the body is not one member, but many (1 Corinthians 12:14).

Today's Thought: The president or general manager may be the leader and the most visible member of the team, but every employee has an important role to play, and every individual is worthy of being valued.

Take a few minutes to evaluate each member of your team. Write down one or more of their primary strengths and at least one area in which you are grateful for their contribution. Make a point of telling each person what you appreciate about them, and how their efforts enhance the success of the business and your department.

Genuine praise brings encouragement to the soul.

Genuine praise brings encouragement to the soul. If you develop a habit of noticing what your employees do well and take time to verbalize your appreciation of their efforts, staff morale will improve and your business team will be strengthened.

Pleasant words are a honeycomb, sweet to the soul and healing to the bones (Proverbs 16:24).

When visiting your field offices, do you make good use of your time?

Scripture: I have sent him to you for this very purpose (Ephesians 6:22).

Today's Thought: Traveling to meet with your staff in other cities is expensive and time-consuming. Plan your time carefully to make the most of your visit. Write an agenda in advance, and provide copies to everyone to allow them time to prepare.

Make your expectations clear, including the results you anticipate and any information you need. Communicate thoroughly any changes in policies and procedures, or important issues that will affect the field office staff.

> If you're traveling from headquarters, remember that you are an emissary from "the top."

If you're traveling from headquarters, remember that you are an emissary from "the top." Allow time to meet with key individuals, to receive feedback, and to keep them in the loop. Before you leave, make sure that your message was heard and understood, and will be acted upon.

Plan your visits well and you will make the most of your travel time and budget.

Like the cold of snow in the time of harvest is a faithful messenger to those who send him, for he refreshes the soul of his masters (Proverbs 25:13).

When we see coworkers fall short, do we offer constructive suggestions?

Scripture: Be subject to one another (Ephesians 5:21).

Today's Thought: You don't have to be a manager to coach and encourage other employees. If you see a coworker being sharp with a customer, failing to follow through, or otherwise falling short, you have a responsibility to the company and the other person to speak up.

We're always to come in a spirit of humility, but that doesn't mean we keep silent. Pick your time carefully, speak to the person alone, and make sure that your comments are kind and constructive.

You don't have to be a manager to coach and encourage other employees.

Simply state what you observed and suggest alternative ways in which the situation could have been handled. Offer your help and invite constructive input from the other person as well. If your counsel is accepted, you will have contributed to your coworker's improvement and to the benefit of the company. If the response is negative or hostile, simply back off and don't be contentious.

Help your colleagues to improve and the whole company will be strengthened.

He is on the path of life who heeds instruction, but he who forsakes reproof goes astray (Proverbs 10:17).

Do you prepare well for new employees?

Scripture: I go to prepare a place for you (John 14:2).

Today's Thought: We know that when we get to heaven, the Lord will be completely prepared for our arrival. We would do well to apply the same principle when preparing to hire a new employee.

Don't wait until the new hire shows up on your doorstep before you put together an orientation plan. Before the employee's first day, make sure that a workspace is prepared, a desk is assigned, the phone is working, and supplies are in place.

Establish an orientation checklist and cover each important item on the first day. Introduce the newcomer to coworkers and key managers, tour the facility, outline the job responsibilities and explain how the work supports the overall results of the organization. Give the new person time to absorb everything, but don't leave him or her sitting around for long periods with nothing to do.

> Don't wait until the new hire shows up on your doorstep before you put together an orientation plan.

Cover all the bases on the first day. Your new employee will feel welcome and will hit the ground running.

To receive instruction in wise behavior, righteousness, justice and equity . . . (Proverbs 1:3).

133

Do you accept defeat easily?

Scripture: But David said to Saul . . . "When a lion or a bear came and took a lamb from the flock, I went out after him and attacked him, and rescued it from his mouth" (1 Samuel 17:34–35).

Today's Thought: One of the bedrock qualities of people who succeed in business is tenacity in the face of adversity, a never-say-die-attitude that seeks to snatch victory from the jaws of every defeat.

If you lose a customer, call and find a way to win back their business. And continue to call on other accounts you want to win. Persistence pays off.

One of the bedrock qualities of people who succeed in business is tenacity in the face of adversity.

If you're having difficulties with equipment or product quality, stay focused on solving the root causes, and follow through until the problem is corrected.

If a key employee quits and leaves behind unfinished business, dig into those files, get yourself up to speed, and complete the project. Whatever the particular problems that you face in your business, tenacious persistence is bound to pay dividends.

Watch over your heart with all diligence, for from it flow the springs of life (Proverbs 4:23).

Do you appreciate and encourage your suppliers?

Scripture: So the craftsman encourages the smelter, and he who smoothes metal with the hammer encourages him who beats the anvil (Isaiah 41:7).

Today's Thought: The smelter works hard to produce the metal that the craftsman uses in his trade. Usually, however, it's the craftsman who gets all the praise. But if the smelter isn't diligent, impurities will be left in the metal, creating weakness that eventually will undermine the craftsman's work.

In some cases, the end result of our work depends more on others than on our own efforts. For example, a waiter cannot serve a good meal if the cook fails to prepare it properly. If we're wise, we will praise and encourage those who support our success by providing the materials and supplies we use to do our jobs. Show a genuine interest in your suppliers' work and express your appreciation for the quality of their efforts. If you do, the work they send you will continue to be first-rate.

Praise and encourage those who support our success by providing the materials and supplies we use to do our jobs.

Then I was beside Him, as a master workman; and I was daily His delight (Proverbs 8:30).

Have you laid the best foundation for your business?

Scripture: Behold, I am laying in Zion a stone, a tested stone, a costly cornerstone for the foundation, firmly placed (Isaiah 28:16).

Today's Thought: Businesses large and small that succeed over the long term usually have several key ingredients in common. One essential element is a solid foundation on which to build.

Strong foundations are centered on three primary pillars: (1) an ethical foundation that governs how business is conducted, including the integrity and quality of the products and services sold; (2) a financial foundation that lays the groundwork for growth and keeps the business from being strangled by cash flow concerns before it can get off the ground; and (3) a performance foundation that includes commitments to hard work, quality, and meeting customer needs.

One essential element for success is a solid foundation on which to build.

Once these pillars are in place, your business will be on a solid foundation for sustained growth.

Do not move the ancient boundary which your fathers have set (Proverbs 22:28).

Do you celebrate your colleagues' victories or are you resentful of them?

Scripture: Rejoice with those who rejoice (Romans 12:15).

Today's Thought: When other salespeople book a big order or land a new account, it's time to celebrate. Do your part to build teamwork and a climate of encouragement by offering your congratulations.

If someone else suggests a new product idea or an improved work process, don't be a wet blanket or a stumbling block; instead, applaud the innovation and jump on board.

Learn from the success of others. Inquire how an account was landed or how the better idea was conceived and apply the same principles to your work. Use others' victories as a catalyst for your own creative thinking, and either come up with your own ideas or help to refine theirs.

Do your part to build teamwork and a climate of encouragement.

Remember, everybody wins when new business comes in and new ideas are implemented. But everyone loses if some people are moping around or backbiting. Join others' celebrations with a whole heart, and you'll soon be celebrating your own success.

Like apples of gold in settings of silver is a word spoken in right circumstances (Proverbs 25:11).

Do you prepare your staff for key initiatives?

Scripture: So Joshua ordered the officers of the people: "Go through the camp and tell the people, 'Get your supplies ready. Three days from now you will cross the Jordan here to go in and take possession of the land'" (Joshua 1:10–11 NIV).

Today's Thought: When the time came to cross into the Promised Land, Joshua delegated responsibility for mobilizing the people to his commanders. In two short sentences he clearly told them what to do, by when, and what the goal was.

> When the purpose is clear and duties have been delegated, it takes only a few words of direction to initiate action.

Use the same model with your staff. When business initiatives come along that require action, call your key leaders together, clearly state the objective, outline what is expected from each staff member, and set a timetable for meeting the goal. Gain agreement and get to work.

When the purpose is clear and duties have been delegated, it takes only a few words of direction to initiate action. Then watch as your key goals are reached.

Listen, for I shall speak noble things; and the opening of my lips will produce right things (Proverbs 8:6).

Do you allow appearances to cloud your judgment when promoting staff members?

Scripture: Do not judge according to appearance, but judge with righteous judgment (John 7:24).

Today's Thought: When identifying candidates for promotion, it is easy to look at appearances, such as how well a person dresses, or if he or she is a smooth talker, or how busy he or she appears when we walk by. However, if we want to make wise decisions, we will look beneath the surface and ask ourselves some key questions:

What is the quality and quantity of the person's work?

> If we want to make wise decisions, we will look beneath the surface and ask some key questions.

Does the person follow through and honor commitments in a timely fashion?

When problems arise, does the person work constructively toward a solution, point fingers, or avoid the situation altogether?

How is the individual perceived by coworkers? Is he respected and looked to for leadership, or is he known to be difficult to get along with?

Don't be swayed by appearances. Look at the whole person, dig below the surface, and your promotions will be on target.

A wise man is cautious and turns away from evil, but a fool is arrogant and careless (Proverbs 14:16).

Do you seek continuous improvement each day in your business?

Scripture: Intelligent people are always open to new ideas. In fact, they look for them (Proverbs 18:15 NLT).

Today's Thought: You've heard the old adage, "If it ain't broke, don't fix it." This is still wise advice in many situations, but some would say, "If it ain't broke, break it, so we can make it better." At the very least, we need to be willing to "break" our habit of staying in the same old rut at work and begin to look for new and better ways to conduct business.

Start by examining your attitude. Do you truly want to improve?

Start by examining your attitude. Do you truly want to improve? If so, evaluate your processes, review your procedures, and identify one or two ways to improve your work. Ask others for suggestions, especially your coworkers and your boss. Be prepared to listen and to implement what you hear.

Adopt a mind-set of continuous improvement and soon you'll be growing and improving your business instead of just running it.

When the grass disappears, the new growth is seen, and the herbs of the mountains are gathered in (Proverbs 27:25).

Do you make snap decisions?

Scripture: Wise people think before they act; fools don't and even brag about it! (Proverbs 13:16 NLT).

Today's Thought: Some businesspeople pride themselves on their snap judgments and quick decisions. But speed is not always a virtue. While many decisions are no-brainers, others require thought if foolishness is to be avoided. Often, it's the words that spill out before we have a chance to think that we later regret.

Develop the habit of stopping for a moment before you weigh in with your opinion or make a decision. First make sure that you understand the full situation— that you've heard all sides and have considered more than your own perspective.

If more time is needed to make a wise choice, don't be goaded into a quick decision. Others will gain confidence in your judgment and decision-making ability when they see you take time for consideration.

Develop the habit of stopping for a moment before you weigh in with your opinion or make a decision.

Think through issues before you take action, and your wise choices will move your business forward with success.

My son, if your heart is wise, my own heart also will be glad; and my inmost being will rejoice, when your lips speak what is right (Proverbs 23:15–16).

Are you able to overcome your mistakes at work?

Scripture: For a righteous man falls seven times, and rises again (Proverbs 24:16).

Today's Thought: All of us will fail at times. But if failure is truly the seedbed of success, we must continue to grow even when it appears that we've been buried by our mistakes. The key is to identify what went wrong, learn how to correct our course, and keep moving forward.

Next time you fall short, don't try to cover it up.

Harland Sanders suffered several business failures, but he continued to persevere until eventually he founded Kentucky Fried Chicken. Likewise, it is said that Thomas Edison failed ten thousand times before he perfected the incandescent light bulb.

Next time you fall short, don't try to cover it up. Be honest about your shortcomings. Ask friends and business associates for insight into what went wrong and for counsel on how to improve. Learn from your mistakes and persevere, and your success will surely grow!

Let your eyes look directly ahead, and let your gaze be fixed straight in front of you (Proverbs 4:25).

Is your leadership focused and under control?

Scripture: Reuben, you are my first-born . . . preeminent in dignity and preeminent in power. Uncontrolled as water, you shall not have preeminence (Genesis 49:3–4).

Today's Thought: Water is a powerful force for harm or good. Properly harnessed, it produces enormous energy and can transport tremendous quantities of goods downstream. However, when it overflows its boundaries it tends to run everywhere, wreaking havoc. The same is true of some business leaders. As long as their power is appropriately channeled, it produces great benefit; out of control, it brings trouble.

> **Focused attention and energy is the most effective power source for your business.**

If you want to make a positive difference in your business today, sit back for a minute and determine where best to channel your efforts. Focus your energy and work in those key areas. Don't respond to every wave and current that might distract you from your primary purpose; instead, move straight ahead toward your goal.

Focused attention and energy is the most effective power source for your business.

It is not good for a person to be without knowledge, and he who makes haste with his feet errs (Proverbs 19:2).

143

Do you realize how your work affects others?

Scripture: Whether a tree falls toward the south or toward the north, wherever the tree falls, there it lies (Ecclesiastes 11:3).

Today's Thought: The phrase "It's none of your business" rarely applies at work, because everything we do on the job affects the people around us. Because every business function is interconnected, the quality and integrity of your work makes all the difference.

Redoing and fixing mistakes always costs more than taking the time to ensure that the work is done right in the first place.

Like a tree that falls in the wrong direction, if your work falls short of meeting customer expectations, the failure will be obvious to all. Redoing and fixing mistakes always costs more than taking the time to ensure that the work is done right in the first place.

Remember, most of the work you do will be passed along to a colleague—or directly to a customer. Do your best work the first time around, and you'll guarantee your long-term business success.

A man will be satisfied with good by the fruit of his words, and the deeds of a man's hands will return to him (Proverbs 12:14).

Did you know that your mistakes often make a bigger impression than your successes?

Scripture: There is no lasting remembrance of the wise man as with the fool (Ecclesiastes 2:16).

Today's Thought: When planning a project, keep in mind that disaster may be far more costly than the gain of a success. Unfortunately, it's often true that our mistakes make a bigger impression than our triumphs. However, don't become paralyzed by risk or fearful of taking action. Instead, weigh the risk against the possible reward, and move forward only when the balance is in your favor.

When a project appears to be failing, analyze the situation and assess the options available.

When a project appears to be failing, analyze the situation and assess the options available for correcting the problem. Once you understand what is causing the lack of success, make corrections and keep moving forward.

If you run out of options and nothing has succeeded, it may be time to give up and cut your losses. Make balanced decisions and know when to quit, and you'll avoid being remembered for your mistakes.

Fools despise wisdom and instruction (Proverbs 1:7).

When should you consider a business merger?

Scripture: There is an appointed time for everything. . . . A time to tear apart, and a time to sew together (Ecclesiastes 3:1, 7).

Today's Thought: In recent years, some blockbuster corporate mergers have grabbed the news headlines. Usually, the focus is on the benefits that the merging parties expect, but trouble often lurks just beneath the surface, waiting for an opportunity to strike. Before you merge your business with another company, consider several key points:

Before merging your company with another, consider the benefits and the risks carefully.

Will the new organization be more effective, or just larger?

Will you be taking on new debt that may be difficult to service?

Is one partner stronger than the other?

How will the combined management team work together?

Before merging your company with another, consider the benefits and the risks carefully, and you will keep your enterprise on track for success.

When you sit down to dine with a ruler, consider carefully what is before you (Proverbs 23:1).

Do you insist upon godly behavior from all your employees?

Scripture: Fear God and keep His commandments, because this applies to every person (Ecclesiastes 12:13).

Today's Thought: As believers in Jesus Christ, we are free to walk in the light of God's commandments by the power of the Holy Spirit at work in our hearts. But what about our non-Christian employees? Considering that God's law "applies to every person," do we hold them accountable to a biblical standard of excellence and integrity?

We can't ask non-believers to act just like Christians in every respect, but we can insist that our staff exhibit truth and honesty when dealing with customers, and that they maintain a professional and kind disposition toward others. Make your standards and expectations clear to all, and set a good example. Then, expect everyone to adhere to your principles.

> **Insist that every employee work in a godly manner, and your business will be blessed by the Lord.**

Insist that every employee work in a godly manner, and your business will be blessed by the Lord.

Lying lips are an abomination to the LORD, but those who deal faithfully are His delight (Proverbs 12:22).

Do you ever take advantage of customers when you have the upper hand?

Scripture: As you have done, it will be done to you. Your dealings will return on your own head (Obadiah 15).

Today's Thought: When you have a competitive advantage in the marketplace or your products and services are in demand, you might be tempted to "gouge" your customers or increase your profits by reducing service levels.

Though profits may increase in the short run, taking advantage of your customers is a short-sighted strategy. Competitors have a way of springing up quickly, and they can take your customers away if you've failed to establish loyalty when you had the opportunity.

Once customers are lost, they're tough to win back, especially if you've squandered your credibility.

Once customers are lost, they're tough to win back, especially if you've squandered your credibility. When you're sitting in the catbird seat, enjoy your success, but don't compromise your integrity or your customers' trust. Always be fair and you'll preserve your advantage for long-term success.

Do not rob the poor because he is poor, or crush the afflicted at the gate (Proverbs 22:22).

Do you pay your workers fairly?

Scripture: For in the way you judge, you will be judged; and by your standard of measure, it shall be measured to you (Matthew 7:2).

Today's Thought: As an employer, you are entitled to a good day's work from every employee. Your staff should be held accountable for providing quality products and excellent customer service. At the same time, however, you have a responsibility to pay fair wages.

Consider the value of each position to the success of your company, not just whether the job is high or low on the totem pole.

To determine an equitable wage scale for each job, conduct a salary survey of other similar businesses—or similar-size businesses—in your area, or check with your industry association. Make sure you place each staff member into the correct salary range.

But don't just take the survey results at face value. Consider the value of each position to the success of your company, not just whether the job is high or low on the totem pole.

If you pay a fair wage, you will hold on to the workers you need to build your business.

He who is gracious to a poor man lends to the LORD, and He will repay him for his good deed (Proverbs 19:17).

Do you believe you can cheat without getting caught?

Scripture: And the LORD will by no means leave the guilty unpunished (Nahum 1:3).

Today's Thought: When a certain business owner occasionally received double payments on accounts or overpayments in error, he developed the practice of keeping the money as additional income. This went on for ten years until one day a buyer approached the owner, offering to buy his business for millions of dollars. The owner thought he had it made, but when the buyers conducted an audit, they uncovered his dishonesty and canceled the purchase.

If you are dealing dishonestly in your business, remember that your sins will find you out.

When the owner asked why they were backing out, the buyers replied, "If you were dishonest all these years with your customers, what else have you lied about? We no longer have any confidence in you or your company."

If you are dealing dishonestly in your business, remember that your sins will find you out. In the end, it won't be worth the price you've paid to cheat. Honesty is still the best policy.

A faithful man will abound with blessings, but he who makes haste to be rich will not go unpunished (Proverbs 28:20).

Do you reward your staff for serving customers?

Scripture: Your shepherds are sleeping. . . . Your people are scattered on the mountains, and there is no one to regather them (Nahum 3:18).

Today's Thought: If you don't have a passion for customer service, your staff won't either, and your customers will eventually leave for greener pastures. But if service is a priority for your business, put your money where your mouth is and develop an incentive system to reward your employees.

First, define great customer service within the context of your business and make sure that every employee knows how to meet the standard. Next, establish a bonus or other inducement for staff members who demonstrate creativity and follow-through on delivering superior customer service.

> **Establish a bonus for those who deliver superior customer service.**

Name an employee of the month, give public recognition for great service, and highlight success stories of employees who met a customer's needs in an outstanding way.

Your staff will focus on those priorities that you reward. Reward excellent customer service and your customers will be well served.

The path of the righteous is like the light of dawn, that shines brighter and brighter until the full day (Proverbs 4:18).

Do you reward your employees for innovation?

Scripture: He has filled them with skill to perform every work of an engraver and of a designer and of an embroiderer . . . as performers of every work and makers of designs (Exodus 35:35).

Today's Thought: In today's competitive business environment, many companies retain their top employees by rewarding them for new product innovations and for developing more efficient processes and systems. Some of the best ideas come from rank-and-file workers who are closest to the action and can see new ways to get the job done.

To foster a climate of creativity, develop an employee suggestion system that offers rewards for ideas that are implemented.

Employee innovation won't happen, though, unless it is encouraged and rewarded. To foster a climate of creativity, develop an employee suggestion system that offers rewards for ideas that are implemented. Respond to every idea, even if it isn't usable, to encourage additional thinking and new ideas. Financial incentives work, but don't overlook the power of praise and public recognition. People like to be paid, but they also like to be appreciated.

Encourage your staff to be creative, and your business will improve by leaps and bounds.

She will place on your head a garland of grace; she will present you with a crown of beauty (Proverbs 4:9).

Do you ask for additional business from your customers?

Scripture: And I say to you, ask, and it shall be given to you; seek, and you shall find; knock, and it shall be opened to you (Luke 11:9).

Today's Thought: An insurance man who was a golfing partner of Henry Ford became upset when he heard that Ford had purchased life insurance from another agent. When he asked him why, Ford replied, "You never asked me."

Often we assume that our customers know everything we have to offer, and that they'll ask if they need one of our other products or services. But most sales are completed only after we take the initiative to ask for the order.

> Often we assume that our customers know everything we have to offer.

Get to know your customer's business. Anticipate how you might expand your service to meet their other needs. When you call on your customers, don't just talk about the business at hand, explain your other offerings and ask for additional business. Look for new opportunities with your existing customers and watch your sales soar.

Two things I asked of Thee, do not refuse me before I die (Proverbs 30:7).

153

Do you keep a steady course at work?

Scripture: Let us run with endurance the race that is set before us (Hebrews 12:1).

Today's Thought: Keep a steady course in business by choosing three action steps each month that will make the biggest difference toward achieving your long-range plans. Each day, focus on work that advances these goals. Step by step, you will stay on track toward meeting them.

Long-range goals are accomplished through short-term actions.

One reason for losing focus is plain old fatigue. Effective managers will maintain a healthy balance at work. Like a marathon runner, who holds a steady pace that can be maintained for miles, you must work at a pace that allows time for rest and leisure.

Save time each week for a date with your spouse, time with the kids, and time alone with the Lord. Schedule it in your planner, and keep your commitments. Run a steady course at work and finish well.

When you walk, your steps will not be impeded; and if you run, you will not stumble (Proverbs 4:12).

Does every part of your business contribute to your success?

Scripture: Every branch in Me that does not bear fruit, He takes away (John 15:2).

Today's Thought: In every organization there will be products, services, systems, and procedures that are no longer efficient, profitable, effective, or worthwhile. The key to maintaining profitability is to as quickly as possible get rid of assets that don't perform well.

Devise a quality control system that periodically appraises the value of each component of your business. Examine your products, review your procedures, and check out your equipment and supplies. Is everything working up to expectation? Is every function still necessary and effective? Is there a better way to accomplish your objectives?

> **If you eliminate the weak areas, you can rechannel your resources into more profitable and successful ventures.**

Every organization has opportunities for improvement. If you eliminate weak areas, you can rechannel your resources into more profitable and successful ventures.

Continually reevaluate your business, making any changes necessary, and your long-term success will be assured.

Where no oxen are, the manger is clean, but much increase comes by the strength of the ox (Proverbs 14:4).

As a business owner or CEO, do you seek outside counsel?

Scripture: She heeded no voice; she accepted no instruction (Zephaniah 3:2).

Today's Thought: Any leader, especially a business owner or CEO, may feel isolated—as if there are no available peers with whom to take counsel. Not just anyone has the experience or qualifications to advise leaders at the top levels of management.

Though qualified counselors may be rare, they do exist. Talk to other business owners to seek out those whose business acumen can challenge or augment yours. Offer your own expertise in a mutually beneficial exchange.

Seek out those whose business acumen can challenge or augment yours.

Share key business issues and decisions, and ask for counsel. When your friends speak, open your ears and be willing to follow their advice. Don't dismiss criticism or downplay constructive insight. You'll no longer feel alone in the battle when you seek wise counsel to enhance your business success.

Without consultation, plans are frustrated, but with many counselors they succeed (Proverbs 15:22).

Are you reluctant to fire people who fail to perform?

Scripture: If anyone will not work, neither let him eat (2 Thessalonians 3:10).

Today's Thought: As manager, it is your job to build a strong business team. If an employee is failing to do the job, doesn't seem to be putting forth much effort, or suffers from "the slows," you need to take prompt action.

First, take the person aside, clarify the requirements of the job, and fully explain your performance quantity and quality of work expectations. Be respectful, but clear and direct.

Follow up your conversation with coaching, and offer praise and encouragement when you see improvement. If the person fails to change, give at least two warnings, preferably in writing, again stating specifically what standard must be met, and by when.

If an employee is failing to do the job, you need to take prompt action.

If the problem persists, your best recourse is to discharge the individual, giving a clear explanation of the reasons and reviewing your efforts to facilitate improvement. Pray that the person learns his or her lesson and doesn't repeat the same mistakes on the next job.

Laziness casts into a deep sleep, and an idle man will suffer hunger (Proverbs 19:15).

Do you move quickly to cut your losses on poor business ventures?

Scripture: The axe is already laid at the root of the trees; every tree therefore that does not bear good fruit is cut down and thrown into the fire (Matthew 3:10).

Today's Thought: Success depends on a willingness to take calculated risks, investing time, energy, and money in an effort to earn a reasonable return. But not every enterprise will prosper. When your results do not measure up to your expectations, it may be time to cut your losses and move on to something more promising or profitable. But how do you know when to pull the plug on a venture?

When your results do not measure up to your expectations, it's time to cut your losses and move on.

Start by identifying benchmarks for measuring expected results. Monitor your progress and if your plan fails, act quickly. Don't waste time second-guessing your decisions or moaning about circumstances. When failure is clear, act decisively and transfer your resources to more fruitful ventures.

Do not love sleep, lest you become poor; open your eyes, and you will be satisfied with food (Proverbs 20:13).

Do you seek to resolve conflicts between coworkers?

Scripture: Blessed are the peacemakers (Matthew 5:9).

Today's Thought: When people work closely together some conflict is inevitable. When a quarrel breaks out in your department, are you tempted to join in or choose sides? Why not play the role of mediator or peacemaker instead?

Successful mediation begins with trust. Nobody will listen to someone who hasn't established a reputation for fairness and integrity. If you've earned the right to intervene, start by looking at the facts of the situation. Ask clarifying questions, designed to elicit truth. Is one person's viewpoint more accurate?

There are always two sides to every story, and reality usually lies somewhere in between. If you can get the parties to consider each other's perspective, you can usually find middle ground where agreement can be reached.

> Nobody will listen to someone who hasn't established a reputation for fairness and integrity.

Keep everyone focused on the goal of reconciliation, not on personalities or past differences. Negotiate an agreement that respects the views of both sides and you will establish a reputation as a peacemaker.

Like an earring of gold and an ornament of fine gold is a wise reprover to a listening ear (Proverbs 25:12).

Could you make better use of your workday?

Scripture: Therefore be careful how you walk, not as unwise men, but as wise, making the most of your time (Ephesians 5:15–16).

Today's Thought: If we allow ourselves to give way to distractions, we will lose focus on our work. Interruptions draw us away from important priorities, hamper our productivity, and increase the chance for errors. To minimize interruptions, plan your work, guard your boundaries, and learn how to excuse yourself politely and return quickly to the task at hand.

To minimize interruptions, plan your work, guard your boundaries, and learn how to excuse yourself politely.

Another way to enhance your productivity is to set three key goals to accomplish each week. Keep a written record of the time spent working on each important task. At the end of the week, look back and evaluate your effort. Determine how much time was focused on the essentials. If your performance fails to match your goals, change your priorities for the next week. Stay focused on the target and your work will hit the bull's-eye!

My son, if sinners entice you, do not consent (Proverbs 1:10).

Are you available to serve your customers?

Scripture: Why was there no man when I came? When I called, why was there none to answer? (Isaiah 50:2).

Today's Thought: Are you too busy managing your business to spend time with your customers? It's easy to get caught up in the urgency of duties and responsibilities and forget about the person who ultimately pays your wages: your customer. If you don't have time for customer service, you need to reassess your priorities. Either delegate some of your work or hire another person to take it on, but don't neglect your customers. They need and deserve your personal attention.

> If you don't have time for customer service, you need to reassess your priorities.

Nothing is more frustrating than not receiving an answer to a problem. Be available to talk, answer your phone, respond to letters and E-mails, and don't hide from customers who have complaints. Treat every complaint as an opportunity to improve your service and solidify your customer relationships.

Serve your customers well and your business will prosper.

He who shuts his eyes will have many curses (Proverbs 28:27).

When making promotions, do you review past performance?

Scripture: He who is faithful in a very little thing is faithful also in much (Luke 16:10).

Today's Thought: Past performance is the best predictor of future behavior. When considering employees for promotion, evaluate their past work objectively. Have they established a reputation for meeting deadlines and honoring commitments? Do they always tell the truth? Do they sound the alarm appropriately when problems arise? Has the quantity and quality of their work always met or exceeded expectations?

Look to the past to make the best promotion for the future.

Never promote someone who has not performed well in the past. Do not allow your personal relationships to influence your decision. Don't succumb to pressure to fill an opening by promoting someone whose performance has been inconsistent. Don't fall into the trap of believing he or she will improve with time. Require improvement in a person's current role before you delegate additional responsibility.

Look to the past to make the best promotion for the future.

Like a bad tooth and an unsteady foot is confidence in a faithless man in time of trouble (Proverbs 25:19).

How do you evaluate your vendors?

Scripture: He who is faithful in a very little thing is faithful also in much (Luke 16:10).

Today's Thought: Before you place a big order or sign a contract with a new vendor, test the supplier's reliability and responsiveness. Start with a trial order before committing all your business. Check out the speed of their deliveries, the accuracy of their counts, and the quality of their service. Does their performance correspond with their promises? Do you uncover any hidden charges or undisclosed costs?

Request a list of the vendor's other customers, and choose several at random to call as references. Ask questions to determine the buyer's satisfaction with the vendor. Do they have any reservations or concerns? Does the supplier respond promptly to inquiries or complaints?

A little due diligence on the front end may save a lot of aggravation down the road.

A little due diligence on the front end may save a lot of aggravation down the road. Determine first if the vendor is faithful, and then arrange for a long-term partnership.

He who walks in integrity walks securely, but he who perverts his ways will be found out (Proverbs 10:9).

Are you a stumbling block to your staff's success?

Scripture: He said to His disciples, "It is inevitable that stumbling blocks should come, but woe to him through whom they come!" (Luke 17:1).

Today's Thought: A key stumbling block for many employees is lack of knowledge about important business matters. As managers, when we withhold information, we are a stumbling block for our staff.

Knowledge is power, and if we want to empower others we must share what we know. Explain your decisions to your staff, including the thought processes that went into those decisions. Not only will this help them understand why you make the decisions you do, it will teach them how to make better decisions themselves.

As managers, when we withhold information, we are a stumbling block for our staff.

Training is another essential component of sharing knowledge. Each week, make a point of discussing one key aspect of your business or department. Help each person move from simple information gathering to comprehension and application of each important principle.

As you share knowledge, your staff's performance will improve, leading to increased business success.

Give instruction to a wise man, and he will be still wiser, teach a righteous man, and he will increase his learning (Proverbs 9:9).

Do you confront your staff when mistakes are made?

Scripture: If your brother sins, rebuke him; and if he repents, forgive him (Luke 17:3).

Today's Thought: When employees err or step out of line, we are obliged to correct them by addressing specifically what needs to be done differently. When contrition is evident, we must be ready to extend forgiveness, provided the person repents.

Keep in mind, however, that saying "I'm sorry" one hundred times is not the same as repentance. True repentance involves both an apology and a change in long-term behavior. Insist on true repentance.

When disciplining employees, follow up by observing their ongoing behavior to verify that the problem has been solved. If the same infraction is repeated, admonish them again and issue a warning, if necessary, that consequences will follow any further transgressions.

> True repentance involves both an apology and a change in long-term behavior. Insist on true repentance.

If you are willing to confront wrongdoing and offer specific correction, you will establish accountability with your staff and improve overall performance.

A wise son accepts his father's discipline, but a scoffer does not listen to rebuke (Proverbs 13:1).

Do you thank your staff every day?

Scripture: And he fell on his face at His feet, giving thanks to Him (Luke 17:16).

Today's Thought: When your employees do a good job, be quick to thank them and remind them of their value to the company. A genuine expression of appreciation will do wonders to improve morale and build loyalty. In addition, when we are liberal with our praise and affirmation, the occasional word of correction will be much better received.

When your employees do a good job, be quick to thank them.

If you really want to build up your staff, think of what you appreciate most about each employee and then tell him or her. A key motivational principle is that you will get more of the behavior you encourage. By demonstrating true appreciation to your staff, you will reinforce their positive attitudes and increase productivity—and your business will become a better place to work.

The crucible is for silver and the furnace for gold, and a man is tested by the praise accorded him (Proverbs 27:21).

Do you regularly ask your employees how you can assist them in their jobs?

Scripture: Jesus stopped . . . and questioned him, "What do you want me to do for you?" (Luke 18:40–41).

Today's Thought: Your staff may be experiencing difficulties or frustrations on the job, or they may have questions that are going unasked and unanswered. The wise manager will create opportunities for these issues to be brought forward before they fester and begin to affect the employee's performance.

When you meet with employees one-on-one, always ask about any obstacles they are facing and if there is anything you can do to help them do their job better. Allow time for them to respond, and don't rush on to the next thing until you have received an answer. Not everyone will raise concerns, but they will appreciate being asked and will value your genuine interest.

Create a climate where employees feel comfortable bringing up their concerns, and they will become more open in asking for assistance.

Ask the same questions at your staff meetings. Create a climate where employees feel comfortable bringing up their concerns, and they will become more open in asking for assistance. If you want to improve your staff's performance, keep asking how you can help.

The glory of kings is to search out a matter (Proverbs 25:2).

Do you ever ask your boss if you can do more to help?

Scripture: Jesus stopped . . . and questioned him, "What do you want me to do for you?" (Luke 18:40–41).

Today's Thought: You can create new opportunities for yourself at work by asking your boss for input regarding your work. If your boss is satisfied with your current effort and output, ask for greater responsibility. Review your work plan with your boss and ask for help in focusing on the most important priorities. Make sure that you're not spending time on work that isn't essential.

Develop the habit of asking how you can help, and you'll help to boost your career.

In addition, ask how you can help your boss with his or her job. Surprisingly, many supervisors are hesitant to ask for help with their own responsibilities, and most will appreciate the gesture.

Develop the habit of asking how you can help, and you'll help to boost your career.

A man's pride will bring him low, but a humble spirit will obtain honor (Proverbs 29:23).

When a competitor attacks your business, how do you respond?

Scripture: Draw for yourself water for the siege! Strengthen your fortifications! (Nahum 3:14).

Today's Thought: When your business comes under attack by an aggressive competitor, circle the wagons around your fundamental strengths and focus on things you can control. For example, are you maintaining effective customer contact? Is product quality being maintained? Are you keeping your commitments to your customers? Are you offering the best possible pricing?

When competition is fierce, nothing will hurt your business more than slipping up on a customer delivery or allowing your pricing to get out of line with the market. Never give your competitors an opportunity of your own making. Many would say the best defense is a good offense, but in reality the best defense is just that—a solid, well-managed defense.

Never give your competitors an opportunity of your own making.

Listen to me and do not depart from the words of my mouth. . . . lest strangers be filled with your strength, and your hard-earned goods go to the house of an alien (Proverbs 5:7, 10).

Are you adaptable in your business?

Scripture: Beat your plowshares into swords, and your pruning hooks into spears (Joel 3:10).

Today's Thought: In today's fast-paced, ever-changing business environment, we must learn how to adapt and overcome obstacles.

Start by investing progressively in the future. Don't get stuck with yesterday's ideas, tools, or technology. Participate actively in business associations, read trade magazines, and attend trade shows and seminars to keep abreast of new trends in your industry. Read business books that alert you to new information and practices.

Learn how to adapt new ideas quickly to enhance customer service, improve product quality, and maximize business efficiency.

Don't rest on your laurels. Plan for action and learn how to adapt new ideas quickly to enhance customer service, improve product quality, and maximize business efficiency. Remember, the best new information won't help you or your business unless you can translate it into action steps that apply directly to your company.

You may not be able to do everything at once, but you can start somewhere now, and begin to adapt your business for future success.

Riches are not forever (Proverbs 27:24).

Do you wait for business to come in the door?

Scripture: Does a bird fall into a trap on the ground when there is no bait in it? (Amos 3:5).

Today's Thought: Business does not usually come to us without some effort. Even referrals are the result of past service. If you want to bolster your business, take a few moments today and determine one action step you can take to obtain some new customers.

Place an advertisement or call a few prospects. For most businesses, generating leads is not a problem. The challenge is following up effectively to turn those prospects into customers.

Review successful past actions that have generated customers, and eliminate steps that were unproductive. Focus your energy, time, and money on proven methods.

> Take a few moments today and determine one action step you can take to obtain some new customers.

Not all ideas cost money—some only require work. Often our best prospects are current customers who can send us more of their business.

Take action today to win a new customer.

So your barns will be filled with plenty (Proverbs 3:10).

How do you select the best possible business partner?

Scripture: Do two walk together unless they have agreed to do so? (Amos 3:3 NIV).

Today's Thought: Too often, business partnerships are based on emotion, temporary convenience, or apparent necessity. Unfortunately, partnerships based on these factors are destined to struggle at best, and often fail.

Effective partnerships are built around a common purpose, compatible values, and agreement on key issues. Before you enter a partnership, determine how much time each partner will commit to the business, how you will divide areas of expertise or focus, and how profits will be invested or shared. Then establish a common business philosophy, and write a comprehensive business plan. Don't skip over key issues or defer them until later; like a marriage, problems will only become worse if not truly resolved up front.

> **Effective partnerships are built around a common purpose, compatible values, and agreement on key issues.**

Time has a way of altering memories, so put every agreement and important principle in writing. Base your partnership on solid points of agreement and you will have the foundation for an effective and profitable venture.

He who is a partner with a thief hates his own life; he hears the oath but tells nothing (Proverbs 29:24).

Do you know when to close a sale?

Scripture: Does a trap spring up from the earth when it captures nothing at all? (Amos 3:5).

Today's Thought: One of the bedrock principles of successful selling is, "Don't forget to ask for the order." If you want to capture new business, you must be prepared to close the sale. To avoid coming up empty, take time before making a sales call to review the benefits of your product or service, apply them to the needs of your customer, and develop a clear and concise sales offer.

Most selling is really a series of small decisions leading up to the "buy" decision.

When you make your presentation, listen to what the buyer says, then outline step-by-step how your product will meet their expressed needs. Confirm understanding and obtain agreement at each step. Most selling is really a series of small decisions leading up to the "buy" decision. Determine each step of the process and lead your customer down the path.

When all the terms have been discussed and agreed upon, ask for the sale and capture the business.

And there will be goats' milk enough for your food (Proverbs 27:27).

Do you brag about what you're going to do before you do it?

Scripture: Does a lion roar in the forest when he has no prey? Does a young lion growl from his den unless he has captured something? (Amos 3:4).

Today's Thought: In every business, there are people who like to talk about their big plans—the mountains they will climb, and the victories that are "just around the corner." But if those goals are never reached, the braggarts soon lose credibility.

It's great to be optimistic and confident, but don't claim successes that have not yet been achieved.

It's great to be optimistic and confident, but don't claim successes that have not yet been achieved. I've often heard salespeople claim that they've landed a big, new account, only to have the business never come in. It's one thing to say that a prospect has made a commitment or is close to signing a contract, but until the fish is in the boat, it's not caught.

Develop a reputation for delivering what you promise, and never promise more than you will deliver. Then when you roar, everyone will listen.

A man will be satisfied with good by the fruit of his words, and the deeds of a man's hands will return to him (Proverbs 12:14).

Do you use all your talents at work?

Scripture: Do not neglect your gift (1 Timothy 4:14 NIV).

Today's Thought: If you have aptitudes and skills that are not currently being put to use in your job, consider how those talents might be beneficial to your employer. If you see possible applications, ask your boss if you can apply your specific abilities, even if they are not directly related to your current responsibilities.

Your manager may be delighted to utilize your talent more effectively, thereby increasing your value to the organization. You may even end up writing your own job description or discovering a new direction for your career—and your job is bound to become more satisfying.

If you find that there's no place to fully utilize your gifts within your present employment, it may be an indication that you should look for a more suitable job elsewhere. It is important to find ways to utilize all of your talents for maximum job success.

> You may end up writing your own job description or discovering a new direction for your career.

A man's gift makes room for him, and brings him before great men (Proverbs 18:16).

Do you hate to turn in business reports?

Scripture: Be diligent in these matters; give yourself wholly to them, so that everyone may see your progress (1 Timothy 4:15 NIV).

Today's Thought: When we faithfully complete assigned reports and paperwork, we achieve three key results.

First, we help our boss and other managers make wise decisions by providing important information, especially if our input applies to long-range planning.

Second, we keep projects on track and make our progress visible. If, by chance, we are off target, timely reporting allows others to correct us before we go too far in the wrong direction. Many projects waste valuable time, energy, and other resources by straying off course without correction.

When we faithfully complete assigned reports and paperwork, we achieve three key results.

Third, we show ourselves to be reliable, industrious, and thorough, which tells our superiors that we can be trusted with more responsibility.

Complete your reports faithfully and accurately for increased success.

A wicked messenger falls into adversity, but a faithful envoy brings healing (Proverbs 13:17).

As a young worker, do you strive to set the best possible example?

Scripture: Don't let anyone look down on you because you are young, but set an example (1 Timothy 4:12 NIV).

Today's Thought: Regardless of your age or level of experience, you have the ability to set a good example for others at work.

Start by presenting a sharp appearance. Dress appropriately and keep your personal grooming habits conservative. You may not feel like "dressing up," but your attire will affect how you are perceived by customers, coworkers, and your boss. Consider the job you'd like to hold in the future, not just the one you have today.

> Demonstrate a desire to improve your work by asking good questions and being willing to learn, adapt, and grow in your job.

Demonstrate a desire to improve your work by asking good questions and being willing to learn, adapt, and grow in your job. Maintain a helpful attitude, especially to your boss and customers. Report to work promptly each day and be reliable with your attendance.

Set a good example and you will be poised for promotion.

She sets about her work vigorously; her arms are strong for her tasks (Proverbs 31:17 NIV).

Do you maintain order among your staff?

Scripture: In those days there was no king in Israel; every man did what was right in his own eyes (Judges 17:6).

Today's Thought: If you want your business to run smoothly and successfully, pay attention to your staff. Make sure every employee is properly trained and knows what is expected. Establish procedures for accomplishing necessary work in a reasonable and productive manner. Set standards for the quality and quantity of work each person should produce, and base your evaluations on quantifiable and objective measures.

> **If you want your business to run smoothly and successfully, pay attention to your staff.**

When circumstances change and work needs to be redirected, make the new direction clear and offer sufficient guidance and explanation. Don't assume that others will know what to do—or why they're doing it—without your input and direction. Things that are obvious to you as a manager may not be obvious to others.

By maintaining orderly systems and giving clear directions you empower your employees for success.

Commit your works to the LORD, and your plans will be established (Proverbs 16:3).

Do you make and keep firm deadline commitments to your boss?

Scripture: Then the king said to me, . . . "How long will your journey be, and when will you return?" So it pleased the king to send me, and I gave him a definite time (Nehemiah 2:6).

Today's Thought: When Nehemiah went to the king and asked to be allowed to go rebuild Jerusalem, he didn't say "I'll be done when I'm done" or "I'll be back when I get around to it." Instead, he promised to finish and return by a specific date.

When your boss gives you an assignment or asks for a report, he or she has every right to expect you to make and keep your deadline commitments. Make sure you understand the project assigned, commit to following through, and then deliver. Establish a practice of meeting or exceeding your boss's expectations.

Make and keep firm commitments.

If you make and keep firm commitments, your boss will appreciate your reliability and will promote you to greater responsibility.

Fear the LORD and the king, my son, and do not join with the rebellious (Proverbs 24:21 NIV).

179

Are your company policies fair to everyone?

Scripture: And God saw all that He had made, and behold, it was very good (Genesis 1:31).

Today's Thought: When God created the heavens and the earth, he established order and designed systems to govern how everything would work together. Likewise, in business we establish orderly systems by developing policies and procedures.

Corporate policies provide a framework for making consistent decisions. Essentially, they specify what we "always do" or "never do" in the conduct of our business. Although designed to be firm, business policies must also be balanced with common sense and propriety when applied to specific situations.

Business policies must be balanced with common sense and propriety when applied to specific situations.

When God completed his work, he was pleased with what he had done. Can you say the same about your company policies? Are they good and fair for everyone? Don't write policies that unnecessarily infringe upon the interests of the three most important groups in your business: your customers, your employees, and the company.

Do not contend with a man without cause, if he has done you no harm (Proverbs 3:30).

Do you truly forgive others when they make mistakes?

Scripture: Put on a heart of compassion; . . . forgiving each other, whoever has a complaint against any one (Colossians 3:12–13).

Today's Thought: When an employee makes a mistake, we must first identify the problem and its source, discuss the consequences of the error for the person and the company, and determine what improvements must occur. Then we must make sure the necessary changes have been made, and that the problem has been solved permanently.

> We must extend forgiveness and not allow past actions to cloud our current attitudes.

When employees understand and acknowledge their shortcomings, and show ability and a willingness to improve, we must extend forgiveness and not allow past actions to cloud our current attitudes. If the person has taken the necessary steps to correct the problem and keep it from happening again, compliment those changes and then move on. Only revisit the issue if the same problem recurs.

Offer genuine forgiveness, encourage positive change, and watch your staff blossom in their confidence and ability.

Stern discipline is for him who forsakes the way; he who hates reproof will die (Proverbs 15:10).

Have you ever lost a star performer who felt unappreciated?

Scripture: I will give you renown and praise among all the peoples (Zephaniah 3:20).

Today's Thought: One of the least expensive and most effective ways to reward your employees is with abundant praise and encouragement. Everybody wants to feel appreciated, especially those who are working hard and producing good results.

Don't assume that your star performers know how you feel, and don't shy away from giving praise because you think it might go to their heads. Tell them how you feel and follow through with other tangible expressions of your appreciation.

> **Everybody wants to feel appreciated, especially those who are working hard and producing good results.**

Furthermore, make sure employees know how they fit into the future plans of the business. Give them a vision for how they can earn promotions, salary increases, and other benefits.

Feeling unappreciated and undervalued is the number one reason why top employees look for other jobs. If you express your appreciation for and share your hopes and dreams with members of your staff, you will build a strong foundation for long-term success.

Pleasant words are a honeycomb, sweet to the soul and healing to the bones (Proverbs 16:24).

Do you maintain a healthy balance in your life and work?

Scripture: Those who wait for the LORD will gain new strength; they will mount up with wings like eagles, they will run and not get tired, they will walk and not become weary (Isaiah 40:31).

Today's Thought: Review the past thirty days. How many hours have you spent at work and how much time have you devoted to family, friends, and quiet time alone with God? Are you running too fast and too far? If you don't have time for balance in your life, you're doing more work than you should.

We all need to run occasionally in our businesses, but even well-conditioned runners stop to rest. To maintain your effectiveness at work, learn when to run and when to rest.

> If you don't have time for balance in your life, you're doing more work than you should.

If your life is galloping out of control, stop. Take time to restore the balance. Learn to delegate responsibility and share the load. Hire another employee so you can reduce your hours. If you get enough sleep, are tuned in to your family, and create unhurried quiet times with the Lord, all aspects of your life will improve.

The spirit of a man can endure his sickness, but a broken spirit who can bear? (Proverbs 18:14).

Do you strengthen your staff by showing concern?

Scripture: He gives strength to the weary (Isaiah 40:29).

Today's Thought: Whether business is booming, times are tough, or everything is status quo, there will be times when your staff grows weary. Be alert for the early warning signs of burnout and fatigue, and be ready to make an investment in your most valuable asset—your people.

When you notice someone dragging or seeming out of sorts, take a few minutes to find out what the issues are and if you can help. Remember to listen before you speak, and don't try to have all the answers. Be sympathetic and encouraging, and reinforce a positive perspective. Genuine care and concern is often the best thing you can offer to someone who is tired or discouraged.

Genuine care and concern is often the best thing you can offer to someone who is tired or discouraged.

Don't drop the ball when the situation starts to improve. Reaffirm your support. When the person is feeling better, take some time to dig into the underlying issues, if possible, in order to alleviate future concerns. Invest in strengthening your staff, and your whole business will be stronger.

It will be healing to your body, and refreshment to your bones (Proverbs 3:8).

Are you working alone and struggling?

Scripture: But woe to the one who falls when there is not another to lift him up (Ecclesiastes 4:10).

Today's Thought: When we're running our own show, it can feel like we've hit a stone wall when problems arise. When you get knocked down, you need other people who will pick you up and get you back on the road to success.

If you're a sole proprietor, or simply work in a place where there's not much interaction with like-minded individuals, gather a group of fellow businesspeople for prayer and mutual support. A good support group is a safe place to share your problems and concerns, discuss key decisions, and find encouragement.

> **When you get knocked down, you need other people who will pick you up and get you back on the road to success.**

Surrounding yourself with experienced businesspeople will help you keep a balanced perspective toward your work. When you're down, others will pick you up, and when *they* stumble, you will be there to lend a helping hand. Band together and watch as everyone's work improves.

If you are wise, you are wise for yourself, and if you scoff, you alone will bear it (Proverbs 9:12).

Do you use work teams in your business?

Scripture: Two are better than one because they have a good return for their labor (Ecclesiastes 4:9).

Today's Thought: Businesspeople talk a lot about teamwork, but when problems arise at work, the temptation is often to try to solve it themselves.

The advantage of work teams is that they bring together individuals with different skills, experience, and knowledge, resulting in a well-rounded effort. As long as team members are willing to work well together and maintain a positive attitude, the output produced by a team will almost always exceed the sum of the individual parts.

> **Work teams bring together individuals with different skills, experience, and knowledge, resulting in a well-rounded effort.**

The key is cooperation. Start by selecting team members who are expert in their respective disciplines and are able to get along. Establish clear goals and expectations, including deadlines and quality standards. Help team members see how their contributions fit with the big picture. Work through differences in style and communication, and keep everyone focused on the ultimate goal. Then watch as your team works together to strengthen your business.

He who trusts in his own heart is a fool, but he who walks wisely will be delivered (Proverbs 28:26).

Do you set reasonable deadlines for your business projects?

Scripture: There is an appointed time for everything. And there is a time for every event under heaven (Ecclesiastes 3:1).

Today's Thought: In your desire to satisfy your customers' needs and expectations, you may commit to deadlines that you later realize you can't keep. You can avoid those situations by planning and communication.

Next time you receive a job from a customer, figure out an accurate time line before you commit to a delivery date. Start by identifying the necessary steps for completion and factor in the work effort required for each step. Check with others to make sure they have sufficient time to do their part, and confirm the availability of any necessary equipment and supplies.

Figure out an accurate time line before you commit to a delivery date.

Next, check your calendar or production schedule. If you see that you are overcommitted, either scale back your other work or ask for a later delivery time. Customers often build in "fudge time," which allows room for negotiation. Plan well and success will follow as you knock out key projects on time.

Forsake your folly and live, and proceed in the way of understanding (Proverbs 9:6).

Do you complete customer requests as promised?

Scripture: That I may finish my course. (Acts 20:24).

Today's Thought: It is a fact of business that customers will contact us with complaints, orders, or special requests. Successful companies insure all customer commitments are met on time and as promised.

Insure all customer commitments are met on time and as promised.

Write down every promise made to each customer. Hand off the request to a team member with a clear explanation of the promise made, the customer's expectation, and time promised for completion. Confirm that the request was understood and will be acted upon.

Write a note to yourself to follow up by placing the note in a date file or on your calendar. Later, check with the assigned person to confirm that the promise was kept as promised.

Lying lips are an abomination to the LORD, but those who deal faithfully are His delight (Proverbs 12:22).

Do you form partnerships with your best customers?

Scripture: Do two walk together unless they have agreed to do so? (Amos 3:3 NIV).

Today's Thought: The best customer relationships are those built on mutual respect and interdependence. When your customers get as much out of their business relationship with your company as you do, everybody wins.

The key to successful partnerships with our customers is agreement. Often, however, we settle for agreement on price and terms alone and never explore deeper possibilities for cooperation. A true customer partnership includes a full understanding of the client's business, a commitment to service and quality levels that meet or exceed expectations, and a willingness to adapt products, services, and business practices to accommodate a client's needs.

> When your customers get as much out of their business relationship with your company as you do, everybody wins.

It all starts with honesty and trust. Meet with your customers, discuss your mutual strengths and weaknesses, and outline a plan for working effectively together. Make sure to reach full agreement if you want a true partnership. If you invest in your customer relationships, they will be lasting and strong.

Keep deception and lies far from me, give me neither poverty nor riches; feed me with the food that is my portion (Proverbs 30:8).

Do you ever lose your cool at work?

Scripture: But the fruit of the Spirit is . . . patience . . . gentleness, self-control (Galatians 5:22–23).

Today's Thought: In the heat of the battle at work, everyone occasionally becomes frustrated and angry. At times like these, any fool can lose his cool and take it out on other people or his surroundings. If we're wise, however, we'll learn how to keep ourselves under control, defuse our anger, and channel it into constructive activity that brings grace to those around us and improvement to the situation at hand.

When the pressure starts to build and you feel your anger rising, take a brief break from the situation to regain control of your emotions. Calmly review your options and proceed with a levelheaded response.

Model and teach proper anger management, and your business will be peaceful and prosperous.

When the pressure starts to build and you feel your anger rising, take a brief break from the situation to regain control of your emotions.

A fool gives full vent to his anger, but a wise man keeps himself under control (Proverbs 29:11 NIV).

Do you coach new employees early in their employment?

Scripture: If a man pampers his servant from youth, he will bring grief in the end (Proverbs 29:21 NIV).

Today's Thought: Sometimes we hire new employees because we're overly busy and need more help. Unfortunately, this often translates into being too busy to properly train and coach our new hires. But if we don't take advantage of those early days when the employee is fresh on the job and can be molded, we may allow bad habits to set in that later will be difficult to change.

A little time invested in training today will save you hours of correction later.

When new employees start, devote the time necessary to provide thorough training. Make expectations clear. Give positive feedback for performance that meets with your standards and prompt correction when work falls below expectations. Don't expect new employees to read your mind. Tell them what they need to know.

A little time invested in training today will save you hours of correction later. Start your staff off on the right foot for business success.

The rod and reproof give wisdom, but a child who gets his own way brings shame to his mother (Proverbs 29:15).

Do you chafe under your boss's authority?

Scripture: Therefore he who resists authority has opposed the ordinance of God (Romans 13:2).

Today's Thought: The Bible makes it clear that God has placed others in authority over us in order to perfect our character and accomplish his purpose in our lives. Consequently, we are to maintain a healthy respect for our superiors at work. We're not to be fearful every minute of losing our jobs, but our boss's power over us should encourage us to turn in reports on time, serve our customers well, and produce the best quality products we can.

Even if your boss is difficult to get along with, you are to submit to his or her authority out of reverence for Christ.

Even if your boss is difficult to get along with, you are to submit to his or her authority out of reverence for Christ. Oftentimes a boss who is hard on you is simply trying to prepare you for greater responsibility and possible promotion by challenging your abilities and testing your resolve.

If you want to succeed at work, respect your boss, submit to authority, and produce reliable results.

The king's favor is toward a servant who acts wisely, but his anger is toward him who acts shamefully (Proverbs 14:35).

When hiring, do you match the candidate with not only the job, but the company?

Scripture: Since we have gifts that differ according to the grace given to us, let each exercise them accordingly (Romans 12:6).

Today's Thought: Two factors are essential for maximum job satisfaction and success: a person's aptitude for the job and how well they fit within the organization.

As a hiring manager, it's important to consider both factors when interviewing applicants. Start by matching the requirements of the job with the candidates' skills and experience. If they have the necessary qualifications, ask questions that will determine their compatibility with your organization. For example, do they prefer business suits or business casual? Fixed hours or flex time? Top-down leadership or self-directed teams?

> Just because someone has the necessary skills doesn't mean they fit your company.

Just because someone has the necessary skills doesn't mean they fit your company. Match well and hire wisely for maximum business success.

Then you will walk in your way securely, and your foot will not stumble (Proverbs 3:23).

Do you promote managers who are able to teach others?

Scripture: The things which you have heard from me . . . these entrust to faithful men, who will be able to teach others also (2 Timothy 2:2).

Today's Thought: Before you promote someone or hire a new manager into a position that requires major staff development, consider carefully whether the person possesses the gift of teaching. Successful instruction, mentoring, and coaching require a good deal of patience. Not everyone has the ability to teach others.

Not everyone has the ability to teach others.

Another important criterion for evaluating management prospects is leadership ability. Can they make difficult decisions objectively, and are they able and willing to take the heat on behalf of their subordinates? Can they grasp the big picture and motivate others to work together for the common good and the success of the organization?

Carefully assess a manager's ability to teach and to lead before promoting him or her to a position that requires these skills. Promote wisely and your business will prosper.

The heart of the wise teaches his mouth, and adds persuasiveness to his lips (Proverbs 16:23).

Do you allow salespeople to snow you with flattery?

Scripture: With flattering lips and with a double heart they speak (Psalm 12:2).

Today's Thought: A time-honored tactic of salespeople who call on our company is to flatter us with our importance, talk up the success of our business, or comment on what astute businesspeople we are.

Don't let flattery get to you. Instead, direct the conversation away from the fluff and back to what the sales representative has to offer. Maintain a pleasant demeanor, but focus on your company's needs and how the vendor can facilitate the best product, price, and service.

Maintain your objectivity and stay focused on your goal. Don't let flattery get to you.

Make it clear what you need—and don't need—from the business relationship, and ask the salesperson to make specific commitments.

Maintain your objectivity and stay focused on your goal, and you will help your company grow and prosper.

With her many persuasions she entices him; with her flattering lips she seduces him (Proverbs 7:21).

How do you handle personal attacks at work?

Scripture: In all things show yourselves to be an example of good deeds ... dignified, sound in speech which is beyond reproach, in order that the opponent may be put to shame, having nothing bad to say about us (Titus 2:7–8).

Today's Thought: The competitive nature of some organizations creates a climate where office politics, personal attacks, and contentious relationships are allowed to flourish. If your company is one where backstabbing and whispering are tolerated, your best defense is to keep your conduct above reproach. Don't give others a chance to slander you.

If your company is one where backstabbing and whispering are tolerated, your best defense is to keep your conduct above reproach.

At first, your efforts to walk in a godly manner may open you to increased criticism, but as you persevere in righteousness and continue to set an example of hard work, gentle speech, honesty, and integrity, your good deeds will put your detractors to shame. Your boss will notice your composure and confidence—and your results—and you will advance in your career.

A gentle answer turns away wrath, but a harsh word stirs up anger (Proverbs 15:1).

Do you delegate key responsibilities to your staff?

Scripture: For this reason I left you in Crete, that you might set in order what remains, and appoint elders in every city as I directed you (Titus 1:5).

Today's Thought: When the apostle Paul established churches in Asia Minor, he delegated responsibility for overseeing those new congregations to some of his trusted colleagues, such as Titus, so that he could move on to the next city and continue his church planting ministry. Even then, he knew that Titus himself could not successfully run every church in the area, so he encouraged him to delegate the responsibility further to a set of elders.

As your business grows and large projects or new ventures come along, build a team of trusted subordinates who can take on increasing responsibilities, and then delegate the authority to them to get the job done. As you equip and empower your employees, you will multiply your own effectiveness and reach your goals more quickly.

> Build a team of trusted subordinates who can take on increasing responsibilities, and then delegate the authority to them to get the job done.

Does not wisdom call, and understanding lift up her voice? (Proverbs 8:1).

Do you follow through on your commitments or are you an empty talker?

Scripture: There are many rebellious men, empty talkers and deceivers (Titus 1:10).

Today's Thought: We've all heard the old saying that "talk is cheap," and nowhere is that more true than at work. It's easy to boast about what we plan to do, but accomplishing key results is another thing altogether. Unfortunately, empty promises will quickly shatter your credibility with your customers and your boss, and others will soon lose confidence in your ability to get the job done.

Focus your energy on producing results and you'll never have to blow your own horn.

Let your good work speak for you. Focus your energy on producing results, and you'll never have to blow your own horn. Support your company's mission and vision, always keep your commitments, and deal honestly with coworkers and customers. As you establish a reputation for reliability, your boss will take notice and entrust you with even greater responsibility.

Do not boast about tomorrow, for you do not know what a day may bring forth (Proverbs 27:1).

Is your staff made up of talkers or doers?

Scripture: Let no one deceive you with empty words (Ephesians 5:6).

Today's Thought: As managers, we may be easily swayed by staff members who talk about their plans and ideas—but do they produce results? We must differentiate between those who merely talk a good game and those who deliver.

Ask subordinates to put their plans in writing, along with a description of how they intend to achieve their objectives. Make sure every goal is measurable and that reasonable deadlines have been established. Then follow up on their promises and hold them accountable for their results.

> **We must differentiate between those who merely talk a good game and those who deliver.**

Don't let talkers off the hook. Take good notes during meetings so that you'll have an accurate record of what has been discussed. Follow up with "memos of understanding" to insure everyone is on the same page.

Coach the talkers and reward the doers, and you'll soon build the best staff possible for your business.

A fool's mouth is his ruin, and his lips are the snare of his soul (Proverbs 18:7).

Do you listen well to your customers?

Scripture: If any man has ears to hear, let him hear (Mark 7:16).

Today's Thought: 3M, a company well-known for its innovative ideas and product improvement, gets many ideas from customer complaints. Part of their secret is that they truly listen to what their customers are saying, and then work to develop useful solutions.

When customers complain, don't become defensive. Instead, see it as an opportunity to improve your products and services.

When customers complain, don't become defensive. Instead, see it as an opportunity to improve your products and services. Most customers want to continue to do business with you. When they raise concerns, pay attention. Listen carefully and take every issue seriously, whether it's direct or implied. Ask follow-up questions to ensure that you understand their full perspective. Let them know that you appreciate their input, and then take appropriate action to solve the problem.

If you will learn to treat customer complaints as opportunities for improvement rather than bristling at the criticism, your products will improve, your customers will stay loyal, and your business will grow.

Wisdom shouts in the street, she lifts her voice in the square; . . . at the entrance of the gates in the city, she utters her sayings (Proverbs 1:20–21).

Do you listen effectively to your staff?

Scripture: Let everyone be quick to hear, slow to speak and slow to anger (James 1:19).

Today's Thought: The further removed we are from the sales floor, customer service, or manufacturing, the more effective listeners we must become to avoid losing touch with the vital pulse of our business. We must develop the habit of truly listening to our staff and heeding what they have to say. We cannot afford to allow our ego, pride, or the sense that we've already "been there and done that" to close our ears to the news from the front lines.

Furthermore, when employees make suggestions for ways to improve the business, we would be wise to consider their perspective and reward their initiative. Learn to listen to your staff and your business will grow as well.

> **We must develop the habit of truly listening to our staff and heeding what they have to say.**

Incline your ear and hear the words of the wise, and apply your mind to my knowledge (Proverbs 22:17).

Do you empower your staff so that they can represent you?

Scripture: If then you regard me a partner, accept him as you would me (Philemon v. 17).

Today's Thought: One of the reasons for having a staff is that you can't be everywhere and do everything yourself. Another reason is to multiply your own productivity.

The best way to maximize your efforts is to train your staff to represent you. Part of effective training and equipping includes delegating responsibility and empowering your subordinates with the authority to make decisions. A well-trained staff will extend your expertise and influence into every area of the company, and will achieve the kinds of results that you desire.

A well-trained staff will extend your expertise and influence into every area of the company.

Supervisors are often unwilling or unable to pass the ball to others, but you will never grow as a manager until you learn how to train up staff to be as effective as you are. Master the art of developing a great staff, and your business will grow like gangbusters.

Like the cold of snow in the time of harvest is a faithful messenger to those who send him (Proverbs 25:13).

When a customer complains, do you fix the root cause of the problem?

Scripture: For this reason we must pay much closer attention to what we have heard, lest we drift away from it (Hebrews 2:1).

Today's Thought: When a customer complains about poor service, a faulty product, or slow delivery, we often rush to resolve the immediate issue but fail to identify and correct the root cause of the problem. Unfortunately, this usually means that the problem comes back.

> We rush to resolve the immediate issue but fail to identify and correct the root cause of the problem.

When your customers raise concerns, take time to dig into the underlying issues and seek to effect a permanent change that will keep the problem from recurring. This may necessitate a revision of your policies and procedures or require more diligence by management to make sure the problem is truly solved. Whatever it takes to solve things once and for all, however, it will be worth it in the long run.

I will render to the man according to his work (Proverbs 24:29).

Do you hold the line with customers who don't pay on time?

Scripture: Reject a factious man after a first and second warning (Titus 3:10).

Today's Thought: Customers that fail to pay on time can kill any business. Most companies that file bankruptcy have demonstrated consistent payment problems with their vendors. If you want your business to succeed, you can't afford to become a creditor to companies that don't pay.

> **If you hold the line on credit, you will avoid holding an empty bag in the end.**

Develop a credit policy that fits and protects your business. Communicate your terms clearly to your customers, and ask for their agreement. Set reasonable credit limits and payment terms, and then hold the line. If payments are late, don't extend additional credit to that customer until their account is brought current.

Switch accounts to C.O.D. if a customer starts to stretch you out, and don't be afraid to drop accounts that consistently fail to meet their obligations. If you hold the line on credit, you will avoid holding an empty bag in the end.

Take his garment when he becomes surety for a stranger; and for foreigners, hold him in pledge (Proverbs 20:16).

Do you need to "win" every point during negotiations?

Scripture: If you make a sale, moreover, to your friend, or buy from your friend's hand, you shall not wrong one another (Leviticus 25:14).

Today's Thought: We've all heard it said that in every negotiation we should strive for a win/win solution. But sometimes, when the discussion gets sticky, we can be goaded into competition rather than negotiation—and then nobody wins.

Remember to always keep the big picture in front of you. When negotiating a contract, make a list of the issues that are most important to you. Prioritize them and identify the impact each will have on your business. Likewise, determine issues that are not as important to you, but which might be important to the other party. Then, when you're sitting at the negotiating table, don't wrangle over points that don't really matter.

> Know when to graciously concede, and you'll maximize your business success.

Know when to graciously concede, and you'll maximize your business success.

Like charcoal to hot embers and wood to fire, so is a contentious man to kindle strife (Proverbs 26:21).

Do you establish policies about things that don't really matter?

Scripture: You shall not oppress a hired servant (Deuteronomy 24:14).

Today's Thought: Because every individual is unique, staff members will operate using different methods. In our efforts to standardize procedures and maintain quality, we may end up establishing policies to govern things that don't really matter. The result is that our employees are demoralized, we end up fighting unnecessary battles, and we run the risk of losing our focus on the things that really count.

> When developing policies and procedures, identify issues that will most greatly affect your customers and your company.

When developing policies and procedures, identify issues that will most greatly affect your customers and your company. If things come down to matters of style or preference, learn to ignore the little things and focus on the desired outcome instead of the steps to get there.

If the right priorities are being accomplished, good results are being achieved, and your customers are well served, celebrate your success and don't split hairs over policies and procedures.

Keeping away from strife is an honor for a man, but any fool will quarrel (Proverbs 20:3).

Do you make positive changes under pressure only to relax your standards when conditions improve?

Scripture: But when Pharaoh saw that the rain and the hail and the thunder had ceased, he sinned again and hardened his heart (Exodus 9:34).

Today's Thought: When God sent the plagues to Egypt, Pharaoh quickly agreed to change his behavior and allow the Israelites to leave. However, as soon as each plague was lifted, he reverted back to his original stubbornness and refused to let the people go. The result each time was more trouble.

When the pressure is on in business, we may step up our performance in response to the crisis. For example, to solve a cash-flow crunch we might begin aggressively collecting our accounts receivable. However, when the storm clouds pass, we often relax and go back to business as usual, as if collections were no longer important.

When you make positive changes to solve a problem, don't stop when the pressure eases.

When you make positive changes to solve a problem, don't stop when the pressure eases. Maintain your focus and intensity, and you won't face the same problems over and over again.

The hand of the diligent will rule, but the slack hand will be put to forced labor (Proverbs 12:24).

Do you find it hard to finish key projects?

Scripture: I have fought the good fight, I have finished the course, I have kept the faith (2 Timothy 4:7).

Today's Thought: When new projects come along, we may get excited and start to work with great enthusiasm. Finishing projects with the same gusto, though, is often a different story. Once the novelty wears off, we must discipline ourselves to continue until completion.

Customers expect a complete job, and they won't be satisfied with anything less.

Even when fatigue sets in and other, newer projects arise, we must resist the temptation to set aside our current, unfinished work and stay on task until the job at hand is done.

Customers expect a complete job, and they won't be satisfied with anything less. Plan well, work diligently, and complete each job to the last detail, and satisfied customers will come back for more.

He who makes haste with his feet errs (Proverbs 19:2).

Do you set a clear vision and direction for your staff?

Scripture: So then, some were shouting one thing and some another, for the assembly was in confusion, and the majority did not know for what cause they had come together (Acts 19:32).

Today's Thought: Every business, large or small, needs a mission statement—a written declaration of why the business exists. From the mission statement, you can then derive a corporate vision, which defines what the business will look like in the future as you successfully pursue your mission.

The mission becomes a rallying point to keep everyone focused on the ultimate goal.

Mission and vision statements provide direction for everyone in the company to define and develop their specific duties and responsibilities. The mission becomes a rallying point to keep everyone focused on the ultimate goal. The vision brings clarity out of confusion, helps your staff stay on track, and keeps everyone working together to serve your customers well.

Put your corporate mission and vision statements in writing, post them prominently in your workplace, and encourage employees to work for their accomplishment every day.

Where there is no vision, the people are unrestrained, but happy is he who keeps the law (Proverbs 29:18).

Are you concerned that you may be embarrassed by your business practices?

Scripture: Then I shall not be ashamed when I look upon all Thy commandments (Psalm 119:6).

Today's Thought: Every business runs the risk of embarrassing itself with its customers, whether it's by being caught with incorrect scanner pricing, failing to honor a warranty, having to recall a faulty product, or otherwise shortchanging the public.

The best protection against embarrassment and shame is to conduct your business with the utmost integrity.

The best protection against embarrassment and shame is to conduct your business with the utmost integrity and deal with problems quickly when they come up. Keep everything above board. In evaluating your policies and procedures, ask yourself, "If our customers could see everything we're doing, would they be pleased?" If not, you have some important work to do.

If you handle every job and serve every customer with diligence and honesty, you will never need to worry that "the truth" may someday come to light.

Differing weights are an abomination to the LORD, and a false scale is not good (Proverbs 20:23).

Do you communicate complete information—good or bad— to your boss?

Scripture: For every breach of trust . . . [he] shall pay double (Exodus 22:9).

Today's Thought: Not giving your boss timely and complete information may cost you twice—not only might you suffer consequences at the moment, but you'll also pay a price in lost credibility. Failure to report problems promptly is a breach of trust, which will undermine your boss's confidence in you. Even failure to share positive news can backfire if your boss perceives that you aren't keeping him or her adequately informed. Nobody likes to hear things through the grapevine that should have been reported directly.

> Even failure to share positive news can backfire if your boss perceives that you aren't keeping him or her adequately informed.

Develop the practice of keeping your boss in the loop, especially when you encounter staff problems, product issues, or an unhappy customer. Your boss may be a valuable resource for improving the situation and preventing further problems.

Let your boss hear the story straight from you, and you'll maintain trust for long-term success.

A man has joy in an apt answer, and how delightful is a timely word! (Proverbs 15:23).

When selecting key staff members, do you insist that they understand today's business environment?

Scripture: Then the king said to the wise men who understood the times . . . (Esther 1:13).

Today's Thought: The times they are a-changin', and so must our perspectives on business. When selecting individuals to hire or promote, first determine whether they understand the current business climate in every respect. Choose only those people who already understand the marketplace, your competitors, and how to attract and keep new customers.

Look for answers that demonstrate a willingness to learn, an ability to adapt, and a desire to grow.

A great interview question to ask candidates is, "What was the most important lesson you learned on each of the jobs you've held over the past ten years?" Look for answers that demonstrate a willingness to learn, an ability to adapt, and a desire to grow.

Ask questions that reveal the person's knowledge and competency regarding important issues that will affect the job, such as technology, marketing trends, or current employment law.

Selecting staff members who understand the times and can adjust to a changing business climate may be the difference between growing successfully and being left in the dust.

Like an archer who wounds everyone, so is he who hires a fool or who hires those who pass by (Proverbs 26:10).

Do you make sure that your staff delivers a consistent level of service?

Scripture: See that you make them after the pattern for them, which was shown to you on the mountain (Exodus 25:40).

Today's Thought: Nothing will undermine a customer's confidence in your business faster than inconsistent quality or spotty service. As a manager, you are responsible for setting a standard of performance and then following up to make sure those standards are maintained.

Develop detailed, written instructions for your staff. Train them thoroughly until they understand your service requirements. Demonstrate how you want the work to be done, and then oversee them to make sure they understand your instructions.

Don't put a new employee on the spot without providing adequate training. Customers don't care if a service failure is caused by a rookie; all they want is results. Set clear standards for customer service and you will improve productivity and customer satisfaction.

> As a manager, you are responsible for setting a standard of performance and then following up to make sure those standards are maintained.

He stores up sound wisdom for the upright; He is a shield to those who walk in integrity (Proverbs 2:7).

Do you maintain a critical eye on your own work?

Scripture: Let each one examine his own work, and then he will have reason for boasting in regard to himself alone, and not in regard to another (Galatians 6:4).

Today's Thought: You have a responsibility to produce your best work each day. Make sure you know what your boss expects, then measure the quality and quantity of what you accomplish. Set a standard for yourself that goes above and beyond expectations, so that your work will be excellent and you will never be caught short.

Set a standard for yourself that goes above and beyond expectations.

Don't wait for your boss to look over your shoulder. Keep your own score. If you fall short, develop an action plan for improvement.

If you take responsibility for your work, setting a high standard and working consistently to maintain your level of production, you'll never have to worry that your annual review will be loaded with surprises. Instead, it will give your boss an opportunity to formally praise your excellent work.

Examine your work, take steps to improve, and let your performance shine like a light.

A wise man is strong, and a man of knowledge increases power (Proverbs 24:5).

Do you carefully review a salesperson's promises?

Scripture: Does not the ear test words, as the palate tastes its food? (Job 12:11).

Today's Thought: It seems that some people will say anything to make a sale. As a buyer, you must evaluate the words of the sales representatives who call on you. Pay careful attention and take notes during sales presentations. Write down important claims and promises, and ask follow-up questions to clarify any unclear points.

Ask how the firm will meet its delivery commitments, and, if appropriate, ask about their service after the sale. How will their products be maintained? Clarify broad statements like "Our product is the best" by asking how claims can be substantiated.

> As a buyer, you must evaluate the words of the sales representatives who call on you.

Once an agreement has been reached, ask for a letter of understanding or a contract that confirms each of the promises made. If you cover your bases here, both you and the seller will know what to expect. The result will be an effective vendor partnership that serves your company well.

. . . to understand a proverb and a figure, the words of the wise and their riddles (Proverbs 1:6).

Are you ready for an audit of your work?

Scripture: Be like men who are waiting for their master when he returns . . . so that they may immediately open the door to him when he comes and knocks (Luke 12:36).

Today's Thought: Every bank branch is subject to an immediate audit without notice. If the audit team walks in at four o'clock, everyone stays until the books balance. Consequently, bank managers know that they have to stay prepared.

If you have everything else under control, you'll be prepared to respond.

Apply the same standard to your area of responsibility and be ready at a moment's notice to give an account of your performance and progress. Tie down loose ends, keep your work current, and quickly resolve any outstanding issues.

Your boss may have a knack for always asking about the one item that isn't done, but if you have everything else under control, you'll be prepared to respond with an action plan. Be ready every day, and you'll welcome your boss's visit.

Do not be afraid of sudden fear (Proverbs 3:25).

Are you ready to serve your customers at all times?

Scripture: Be dressed in readiness, and keep your lamps alight (Luke 12:35).

Today's Thought: The most successful businesses are those that focus their efforts on satisfying their customers' needs and convenience. It sounds simple, but it's amazing how many companies appear as if they haven't given their customers a single thought.

Keep track of what your customers request, and buy and maintain adequate inventory levels so that you can always say, "Yes, we have that in stock."

> It's amazing how many companies appear as if they haven't given their customers a single thought.

Hire and schedule enough employees to keep an appropriate staffing level so that your customers don't have to wait forever. Establish your business hours to satisfy your customers' convenience.

If you're not ready to serve your customers, someone else will. You may lose your customers forever if you are not prepared to meet their needs.

Prepare your work outside, and make it ready for yourself in the field; afterwards, then, build your house (Proverbs 24:27).

Do you carry out company directives faithfully?

Scripture: Did not Moses give you the law, and yet none of you carries out the law? (John 7:19).

Today's Thought: Difficult or complex business decisions will come our way each day. We may have to decide whether to accept returned merchandise without a receipt, extend credit to a marginal customer, or implement an unpopular human resources policy. Unless we're being asked to do something illegal or in violation of God's higher law, we are responsible to carry out the letter and the intent of company policies and directives, even if we don't agree with them.

If you disagree with a company policy, talk to your boss and suggest a positive change.

Many major mistakes are made by employees who decide they know better than the company and thus choose to ignore standing directives. If you disagree with a company policy, talk to your boss and suggest a positive change. If you work through the proper channels, your idea may become policy.

Make yourself a successful team player by faithfully following through with your responsibilities and upholding company policy.

Where there is no vision, the people are unrestrained, but happy is he who keeps the law (Proverbs 29:18).

When considering a job offer, do you look at more than salary and benefits?

Scripture: Do not judge according to appearance, but judge with righteous judgment (John 7:24).

Today's Thought: Before saying yes to a job offer, answer the following questions:

Does the firm have a good reputation in the market? Is management honest and forthright?

Do you understand and agree with the company's mission statement? Are you excited about the firm's products or services?

How well will you fit in? A "free spirit" may not mesh well with an old-line conservative company. Even if your skills and experience perfectly match the job description, you are likely to become unhappy if you don't fit well with the corporate culture.

Look before you leap and you will enhance your prospects for long-term success on the job.

Finding the right job involves careful consideration of every aspect of a company and how well they correspond with your skills, experience, interests, and personality. Look before you leap and you will enhance your prospects for long-term success on the job.

How blessed is the man who finds wisdom, and the man who gains understanding (Proverbs 3:13).

219

Do you ever see a problem at work, but choose to remain quiet?

Scripture: When he is a witness, whether he has seen or otherwise known, if he does not tell it, then he will bear his guilt (Leviticus 5:1).

Today's Thought: A restaurant employee observed a cook who was ignoring health department rules in violation of a clear management directive. He chose to say nothing, allowing the unsanitary practice to continue. When the health inspector made an unannounced visit, the violation was discovered and the restaurant was cited and placed on probation, resulting in a rash of unwanted publicity.

Our loyalty must be to protect the interest of our employer. Speak up!

When we see a problem in our company or believe that a customer is unsatisfied, we have a duty to make the matter known. We might prefer to avoid the trouble of bringing it up, or perhaps we secretly desire to see a colleague fail, or we may be afraid of being wrong. Nevertheless, our loyalty must be to protect the interest of our employer. Speak up!

A false witness will perish, but the man who listens to the truth will speak forever (Proverbs 21:28).

Do you gloat about a smashing victory over a competitor?

Scripture: Yes, you, do not gloat over their calamity in the day of their disaster (Obadiah v. 13).

Today's Thought: When you win a major bid or take a customer away from a competitor, enjoy the victory but don't gloat. Gloating leads only to overconfidence and may well kindle anger and retaliation from your competitor.

In the past, one particular rival repeatedly gloated over taking a large account away from my firm. After a while, I established a designated file with the names of all my competitors' accounts, which I then made a special project of working to obtain. As a direct result of their smug attitude, I worked their prospects harder.

Focus your enthusiasm and energy on serving your new customer.

When you do land a big account, recognize that your work is just beginning. Instead of gloating, focus your enthusiasm and energy on serving your new customer and obtaining the next one.

Pride goes before destruction, and a haughty spirit before stumbling (Proverbs 16:18).

221

Do you take notes during meetings?

Scripture: Write in a book what you see (Revelation 1:11).

Today's Thought: How often have you sat through a meeting, listening carefully but not writing down key points, and then failed to follow through on something important? If your boss or a customer takes the time to tell you something, it's worth writing down the information.

When the Lord gave the apostle John a vision of the end times, he instructed him to write what he observed, because he knew that otherwise John couldn't remember everything.

To increase your effectiveness, take good notes during meetings.

Time will cause your memory to fade, and may "rewrite" important details. To increase your effectiveness, take good notes during meetings, both on informational and action items. Then transfer your action items to a "things to do" list or assign tasks to your staff.

As you take notes—and then take action—you will be amazed by the improvement in your accuracy, effectiveness, follow-through, and results.

Have I not written to you excellent things of counsels and knowledge, to make you know the certainty of the words of truth that you may correctly answer to him who sent you? (Proverbs 22:20–21).

If you're traveling, on vacation, or changing jobs, have you left a map for others to follow?

Scripture: I will also be diligent that at any time after my departure you may be able to call these things to mind (2 Peter 1:15).

Today's Thought: If a customer calls when you're out of the office, can your coworkers find the information they need to serve your customer's needs? You can make your business run more smoothly, and increase your chances for promotion, by making it easy for others to do your job.

Take the time to write clear, concise procedures covering each of your responsibilities. Keep an index of where to find key documents, and maintain a list of key contacts. Make your staff aware of these resources, and encourage them to use this information when you are not available.

If you organize and document your job duties, you'll both increase your company's effectiveness and enhance your stature in the eyes of management.

> You can make your business run more smoothly, and increase your chances for promotion, by making it easy for others to do your job.

Give instruction to a wise man, and he will be still wiser, teach a righteous man, and he will increase his learning (Proverbs 9:9).

Are you ever slow to pay employee wages or payroll taxes?

Scripture: The wages of a hired man are not to remain with you all night until morning (Leviticus 19:13).

Today's Thought: Every business has a moral responsibility to ensure that all wages are paid promptly—and that includes making payroll tax withholding payments to the government.

If your business is short of cash, do everything you can to make your payroll (and tax) payments on time. Payroll delays can be catastrophic. Employee morale and confidence will plummet, and you may lose some of your best people to other companies Also, if you fail to make timely payments to the IRS, the interest and penalties will mount quickly on the unpaid taxes, further crippling your business. Once you get behind, it's even harder to catch up.

Establish a payment plan with payroll as your number one priority.

Develop a plan to accumulate cash reserves in order to ease the crunch when business is slow. Establish a payment plan with payroll as your number one priority. Pay all wages promptly to preserve your greatest asset—your employees.

I walk in the way of righteousness, in the midst of the paths of justice, to endow those who love me with wealth (Proverbs 8:20–21).

Do you make accommodations for employee disabilities?

Scripture: You shall not . . . place a stumbling block before the blind (Leviticus 19:14).

Today's Thought: Current law requires employers to make reasonable accommodations for workers with disabilities, but Scripture has always instructed us to help those who are disadvantaged and to care for those in need.

Not only is caring for the disadvantaged biblical, it makes a lot of practical sense as well. Just because an individual has a certain disability doesn't mean they can't do other tasks extremely well. When we assist those with special challenges, we may obtain a star employee who has been overlooked by others.

Scripture has always instructed us to help those who are disadvantaged and to care for those in need.

Evaluate job openings with an eye toward making an opportunity available to someone with a disability. Consider the job requirements, look carefully at the person's qualifications, and consider how the prospective employee might fit in.

If you look for ways to follow God's principle of caring for the disadvantaged, you will obtain the staff you need and create loyal employees who will enhance your long-term success.

She extends her hand to the poor; and she stretches out her hands to the needy (Proverbs 31:20).

Do you ever speak critically about your competitors?

Scripture: You shall not go about as a slanderer among your people (Leviticus 19:16).

Today's Thought: In the heat of the battle to get a new account you may be tempted to spread negative gossip and attack the competition. But tearing others down is never the best way to build yourself up. Spreading rumors will only cause you to lose credibility.

Tearing others down is never the best way to build yourself up.
The best strategy in marketing and sales is always to focus on your own strengths. If your competitors have areas of obvious weakness, identify your company's strength in that area and talk about that instead. If the competition is slow on delivery, emphasize your dependability and speed. If staff turnover is a problem for your rival, focus on the stability of your staff. Selling your strengths is a surefire recipe for success.

He who conceals hatred has lying lips, and he who spreads slander is a fool (Proverbs 10:18).

Do you respect older workers or treat them like old fogies?

Scripture: You shall rise up before the grayheaded, and honor the aged (Leviticus 19:32).

Today's Thought: In the fast-paced world of Internet access, dot.com millionnaires, and high-stakes global competition, young hotshot owners and managers may think they have all the answers, and that older workers are irrelevant.

However, even though rapidly emerging technologies may pose a challenge to even the most energetic business veteran, the lessons they've learned over time can give invaluable help and perspective to their younger colleagues.

As I came up through the ranks in business, there were times I didn't listen to the voice of experience, and I paid a big price. There were also times I managed to avoid some major elephant traps when I did heed some sage advice.

No matter how "cutting edge" your business might be, you're wise if you seek out experienced counsel and and listen to it. You will profit from others' experience instead of paying the same price yourself.

No matter how "cutting edge" your business might be, you're wise if you seek out experienced counsel and listen to it.

The glory of young men is their strength, and the honor of old men is their gray hair (Proverbs 20:29).

When you promote a leader, do you make your expectations clear?

Scripture: Charge Joshua and encourage him and strengthen him; for he shall go across at the head of this people (Deuteronomy 3:28).

Today's Thought: When naming new managers, it is important to charge them with clear responsibilities and invest them with the necessary authority to do the job well.

Charge new managers with clear responsibilities and invest them with the necessary authority to do the job well.

Outline your expectations, and establish clear, objective, and measurable goals. Discuss the personal conduct attendant to the job, especially if the person is being promoted from among the ranks, and clarify any other key factors. Then communicate your support of the manager to his or her staff and subordinates.

Once you have developed objective responsibilities and established clear lines of authority, you will have a firm foundation for holding the new supervisor accountable, and your manager will be primed for success.

By wise guidance you will wage war, and in abundance of counselors there is victory (Proverbs 24:6).

Do you support your new managers?

Scripture: Charge Joshua and encourage him and strengthen him; for he shall go across at the head of this people (Deuteronomy 3:28).

Today's Thought: When promoting people to management positions, don't turn them loose without providing encouragement and ongoing support. Identify and continue to build on the leadership skills and aptitudes that caused you to place your trust in the new manager.

At the same time, pay attention to areas of weakness that need to be strengthened, and develop a plan for helping the manager improve.

New managers need and deserve extra support until they learn the ropes.

Make sure you have furnished proper training and direction to establish a proper foundation for their performance. Then follow up regularly, inquiring as to what challenges they are encountering and making suggestions for how those obstacles may be overcome.

Remember that new managers need and deserve extra support until they learn the ropes. Encourage, train, and mentor your new managers and they will bring success to your business.

Heed instruction and be wise, and do not neglect it (Proverbs 8:33).

Do you know when to break out of your routine?

Scripture: And the LORD spoke to [Moses] saying, "You have circled this mountain long enough. Now turn north" (Deuteronomy 2:2–3).

Today's Thought: One definition of insanity is "continuing to do the same things, but expecting different results." In business, it's easy to get in a rut following routines and established practices. When you have given a good effort to an initiative but gotten nowhere, if you are treading water or going in circles, it's time to break out, change directions, try something bold and new.

Break out of your rut and forge a new direction for business success.

Stop long enough to determine what kind of change will bring the best results, then break the circle. If the new direction goes nowhere, stop and rethink your position. But if you are making progress, press on and keep the momentum going.

If you're not willing to change, you'll get nowhere. Break out of your rut and forge a new direction for business success.

When you walk, your steps will not be impeded; and if you run, you will not stumble (Proverbs 4:12).

230

Do you fulfill your handshake agreements as well as your contracts?

Scripture: If a man makes a vow . . . or takes an oath to bind himself with a binding obligation, he shall not violate his word (Numbers 30:2).

Today's Thought: It used to be, when negotiating contracts and agreements, that a deal was a deal. Period. A person's handshake was as binding as a signature on the bottom line. But some businesspeople and companies today are expert at creating and using legal loopholes to alter or avoid contractual agreements. Such practices make everyone wary and undermine trust in relationships.

Honor all your commitments.

Conduct your business according to the integrity of your word. When striking an agreement, keep the terms simple and understandable to all—and follow through on every detail. It's better not to promise than to promise and not deliver. Your word does matter.

Honor all your commitments. Your vendors will love you and your customers will keep coming back.

A good name is to be more desired than great riches, favor is better than silver or gold (Proverbs 22:1).

When you ask your customers for feedback, do you really listen to their answers?

Scripture: Hear my words, you wise men, and listen to me, you who know (Job 34:2).

Today's Thought: When shopping or eating in a restaurant, have you ever been asked "Are you finding everything okay?" or "How is everything?" but it was clear that the person asking the question couldn't have cared less about your reply?

It's better not to ask, than to ask and not care about the answer.

It's better not to ask, than to ask and not care about the answer. In your business, when you ask a customer if everything is okay, stop for a second, look the person in the eye, and tune in to their response.

Give the customer time to answer the question fully. If a concern is raised, deal with the issue without becoming defensive or argumentative. Whether the response is positive or negative, thank the customer for taking time to share his or her perspective.

Listen to your customers and your business will grow.

Now therefore . . . listen to me, and pay attention to the words of my mouth (Proverbs 7:24).

Are you looking in the right places for new business?

Scripture: Do horses run on rocks? Or does one plow them with oxen? (Amos 6:12).

Today's Thought: No one would plow solid rock in order to plant crops. Instead, you would look for a field that already has rich, fertile soil. When seeking to increase your business, apply the same principle: Work the fertile ground.

Often the best place to plant new seeds is with your current customers, because the hard work of tilling the soil has already been done. Your customers will appreciate the personal attention, and you will earn their loyalty.

When seeking to increase your business, work the fertile ground.

Look for ways to increase your sales by rewarding existing customers with bonuses such as frequent dining cards, additional discounts, or special recognition. Ask repeat buyers what you can do to earn even more of their business.

When you work the fertile ground of your current customers, your sales will increase and your business will grow.

She considers a field and buys it; from her earnings she plants a vineyard (Proverbs 31:16).

Do you set clear quality standards for your staff to meet customer expectations?

Scripture: And the LORD said to me, "What do you see . . . ?" And I said, "A plumb line" (Amos 7:8).

Today's Thought: A plumb line is used to establish an absolutely true vertical line, an important standard when building straight walls, for example. Likewise, in our businesses, we must develop and maintain standards of quality that help us meet our customers' expectations. Otherwise, they are likely to leave for our competitors.

Focusing on quality brings its own rewards: improved customer satisfaction and growth in your business.

Evaluate your company and then set clear, quantifiable, high-quality standards for everything your business does. Train your staff to pursue quality improvement relentlessly, and insist that they follow through every time.

As a manager, it's your job to ensure that these key standards are met and to make adjustments when your products and services are "out of plumb."

Focusing on quality brings its own rewards: improved customer satisfaction and growth in your business.

I have directed you in the way of wisdom; I have led you in upright paths (Proverbs 4:11).

How do you react when employees make mistakes out of ignorance?

Scripture: And now, brethren, I know that you acted in ignorance" (Acts 3:17).

Today's Thought: In Acts 3, Peter addresses a crowd that has gathered in amazement at the healing of the lame beggar. First, he acknowledges that the people are ignorant of the truth about Jesus Christ, and then he proceeds to teach them about repentance and salvation.

When mistakes occur in your business, give the other person the benefit of the doubt. If the error was made in ignorance, handle the situation calmly. Venting your frustration won't help, especially if the employee genuinely didn't know better.

If you treat mistakes as learning opportunities, your staff will grow and become more productive.

Clarify the circumstances, explain the results of the error, and teach the employee how to avoid the problem the next time a similar situation arises. If possible, allow the person to redo the work and repair the damage.

If you treat mistakes as learning opportunities, your staff will grow and become more productive.

Do not go out hastily to argue your case; otherwise, what will you do in the end, when your neighbor puts you to shame? (Proverbs 25:8).

Do you pass up opportunities and miss the boat?

Scripture: The stone which the builders rejected has become the chief corner stone (Psalm 118:22).

Today's Thought: If we restrict our thinking to conventional means, we may miss tremendous opportunities. In your business, look for new ways to use existing resources to generate additional income or cut costs.

Evaluate the by-products of your business to make sure you are not wasting money or missing an opportunity to expand your revenue.

For example, a retail chain saved money by burning wood delivery pallets instead of paying for disposal. In another instance, a junkyard operator increased his profits by developing a process for separating non-magnetic metal from shredded auto bodies.

Evaluate the by-products of your business to make sure you are not wasting money or missing an opportunity to expand your revenue. Look for one way to change your thinking about waste and "extras" that might turn a losing venture into a winner.

Each piece of "rejected stone" that you can find a use for will add to your bottom line.

The badgers are not mighty folk, yet they make their houses in the rocks (Proverbs 30:26).

Are your sales efforts focused in the right direction?

Scripture: Do horses run on rocks? Or does one plow them with oxen? (Amos 6:12).

Today's Thought: When making sales calls, don't just run around trying to make the most contacts. Instead, take time to properly qualify your prospects and focus on calling the best ones. Just as a horse will slip and fall when galloping over rocks, you will stumble in your sales efforts if you run off without considering your path.

Choose your trails carefully and you will surely reach your destination.

Before you pick up the phone or hit the streets, research your prospect's business and determine how your product best fits their needs. Call potential customers in advance to learn more about their needs, and establish a relationship with key contacts. Then carefully map out a territory and make your best presentation.

Choose your trails carefully and you will surely reach your destination. You won't slip as you spend your energy effectively obtaining new business.

So you will walk in the way of good men, and keep to the paths of the righteous (Proverbs 2:20).

237

Do you look for business opportunities missed by others?

Scripture: So she departed and went and gleaned in the field after the reapers (Ruth 2:3).

Today's Thought: When starting a new venture, one key to success is to find a niche market not currently being serviced and focus your energies there. Wal-mart got its start by servicing small communities that were being ignored by the larger chain stores. Today, Wal-mart is the largest chain store of its kind.

What opportunities are "left lying in the field," waiting to be gleaned?

In your current or proposed market or industry, are there needs going unmet? What slice of business can you obtain? Who is currently serving that market? Is your location better than your competitor's? How can you redefine the market to gain a competitive advantage? What opportunities are "left lying in the field," waiting to be gleaned?

Will he not render to man according to his work? (Proverbs 24:12).

Do your employees "buy in" to your business vision?

Scripture: And the king stood by the pillar and made a covenant before the LORD. . . . And all the people entered into the covenant (2 Kings 23:3).

Today's Thought: Effective leadership includes developing a clear company mission and vision, with achievable goals to measure progress and success. The next important step is to get your staff to enter into your mission and vision.

It isn't enough simply to explain the corporate plan; your employees must be given an opportunity to embrace it. Start by enlisting the support of your managers and supervisors. Without unified support for your vision, they will not be working together toward a common purpose, which will only result in dissension and distraction.

Make your vision easy to grasp and your employees will take ownership of the process.

Start by boldly stating your plan and ask your staff to respond with suggestions for implementation and follow-through. Make your vision easy to grasp and your employees will take ownership of the process. The resulting unity of purpose will bring success to your business.

Surely there is a future, and your hope will not be cut off (Proverbs 23:18).

Is your equipment in good repair to serve your customers' needs?

Scripture: Jehoshaphat made ships of Tarshish to go to Ophir for gold, but they did not go for the ships were broken at Ezion-geber (1 Kings 22:48).

Today's Thought: According to Murphy's Law, anything that can go wrong, will go wrong—and at the worst possible moment. One antidote is to keep important tools, software, and machinery in good repair at all times.

If your equipment is showing signs of wear or requires ongoing maintenance, don't wait. Place that service call now.

Keep your equipment shipshape for long-term success.

If your computers are running sluggish, upgrade now. Don't wait for a crash to occur when you can least afford it. If your delivery truck is burning oil, get it into the shop now before a breakdown stops all deliveries.

Making a priority of upgrades and maintenance is an investment in the future. Keep your equipment shipshape for long-term success.

She looks well to the ways of her household, and does not eat the bread of idleness (Proverbs 31:27).

When pursuing a key goal, do you go in a straight line?

Scripture: Asahel pursued Abner and did not turn to the right or to the left (2 Samuel 2:19).

Today's Thought: Unless you are climbing a rock face, the quickest path to a goal is usually a straight line. In business, we are often tempted to be diverted, waylaid, or distracted from pursuing our goals with single-minded intent. But every delay costs time and money, and the quicker we reach an important goal, the sooner we reap the rewards of our achievement.

> Unless you are climbing a rock face, the quickest path to a goal is usually a straight line.

Start with an explicit statement of your mission and vision. When the purpose is clear and compelling, it's easier to stay focused on the goal. Next, develop an action plan that will help you accomplish your goals. Establish "mile markers" so you can gauge your progress. Then get busy! Once you are on track and moving, your success will be quick and sure.

Folly is joy to him who lacks sense, but a man of understanding walks straight (Proverbs 15:21).

When evaluating the competition, do you monitor trends carefully?

Scripture: David grew steadily stronger, but the house of Saul grew weaker continually (2 Samuel 3:1).

Today's Thought: Most companies don't rise or fall overnight. The outcome may suddenly become clear one day, but the underlying causes have usually been in place for months or years.

No matter which way the barometer is moving, watch the trends, act quickly, and your business will stay on top.

If you are losing ground to a competitor, act quickly to shore up your weaknesses and find new ways to build on your strengths. Identify the root causes of the slide, and establish a plan to turn the tide. Move quickly and decisively. If the trend is downward, time is not on your side.

The same principles apply on the upward side. If you identify a competitive advantage, move quickly to make the most of it. Identify the core strengths of your business, and develop a plan to maximize your return on investment.

No matter which way the barometer is moving, watch the trends and act quickly, and your business will stay on top.

Good understanding produces favor (Proverbs 13:15).

Do you listen carefully to warnings?

Scripture: Nevertheless, the people refused to listen to the voice of Samuel (1 Samuel 8:19).

Today's Thought: Businesses rarely lose customers suddenly or for no reason. Most customers will warn us of their concerns, or send signals of their dissatisfaction, before they leave for another supplier.

The key to keeping your customers is to pay attention to what they are saying. When you receive negative feedback, gripes, or even pointed humor, take the issue seriously. Get personally involved, ask questions, and identify the seriousness of any problems.

Once you are certain that you understand the situation, take appropriate action to address the customer's concerns. Follow up with the customer to make sure that the issue was resolved to his or her complete satisfaction.

Stop small complaints from growing into big problems.

Don't wait for the handwriting on the wall. Stop small complaints from growing into big problems. Keep your customers happy and your business will stay on top.

A man will be praised according to his insight, but one of perverse mind will be despised (Proverbs 12:8).

Do you act as if you can run your business forever?

Scripture: Set your house in order, for you shall . . . not live (2 Kings 20:1).

Today's Thought: Nobody can operate a business forever, but many owners act as if they will be the exception to the rule. Even when they become ill, some owners refuse to consider transferring their business to others.

The reason for such lack of foresight may be denial, pride (believing that no one could possibly succeed us), or pure willfulness. Unfortunately, failure to develop a plan of succession often puts the owner's family and employees at risk.

Failure to develop a plan of succession often puts the owner's family and employees at risk.

Wise and prudent owners accept the inevitable reality that they can't carry on forever, and they plan to either sell the business or appoint and train a successor. Even when succession plans are in place, the transfer of ownership and control from one generation to the next is a tricky proposition. But one thing is for certain: Failure to plan is a guaranteed plan for failure.

The naive inherit folly, but the prudent are crowned with knowledge (Proverbs 14:18).

When hiring, do you make sure key staff members share your vision?

Scripture: The LORD has sought out for Himself a man after His own heart (1 Samuel 13:14).

Today's Thought: To be successful, any organization must work as a team. The most effective team players will share a common vision with the leader.

When hiring new staff members, clearly outline your mission and vision and ask for the applicant's feedback. Listen carefully to the response and look for genuine agreement, excitement, and interest. If you sense that the applicant "doesn't quite get it" or is not in synch with your vision, back off and don't hire that person, regardless of his or her other qualifications. Even the most gifted individuals will not fit in if they can't embrace the corporate vision wholeheartedly.

> **When team members are truly united around a common purpose, a synergy develops that transcends the sum of the individual parts.**

When team members are truly united around a common purpose, a synergy develops that transcends the sum of the individual parts. Build your team carefully around your vision, and your business will soar.

The locusts have no king, yet all of them go out in ranks (Proverbs 30:27).

Does your quality-control system focus on the little things?

Scripture: Now a certain man drew his bow at random and struck the king of Israel in a joint of the armor (1 Kings 22:34).

Today's Thought: Pay attention to detail in your quality-control procedures. Even small weaknesses may result in major product or service failures that will affect your customers.

When problems surface, don't assume they are isolated and can't happen again. Neither should you dismiss problems as minor and thereby fail to take corrective action. As the king of Israel discovered too late, even small openings in the armor can be fatal.

Pay attention to the little things, and your business will enjoy ongoing success.

Evaluate your systems and processes, and repair any weaknesses or holes. Use your company's products and services yourself. Develop procedures to solicit honest feedback about quality from your customers. Pay attention to the little things, and your business will enjoy ongoing success.

For the waywardness of the naive shall kill them, and the complacency of fools shall destroy them (Proverbs 1:32).

When asked your opinion at work, do you always chime in, or do you speak up only when you have useful information?

Scripture: Who is this that darkens counsel by words without knowledge? (Job 38:2).

Today's Thought: When your boss or a coworker asks for information or a solution to a problem, don't feel pressured to have all the answers. Slow down and take time to organize your thoughts.

If you do have the solution, speak up. If you don't know the answer, or you need more information before you can respond, ask pertinent questions to determine the exact information that is needed. Whatever you do, don't ramble on just to say something. Unless you can offer solid, useful information, it's better to remain quiet.

Learn to speak only when you have useful information, and others will appreciate your wisdom.

I once had a teacher who gave out minus points for irrelevant information. I quickly learned to leave a space blank on a test rather than try to bluff an answer.

Learn to speak only when you have useful information, and others will appreciate your wisdom.

Righteous lips are the delight of kings, and he who speaks right is loved (Proverbs 16:13).

Do you devise magnificent plans, but struggle to finish your projects?

Scripture: Thus Solomon finished the house of the LORD and the king's palace, and successfully completed all that he had planned (2 Chronicles 7:11).

Today's Thought: A lot of managers have great plans. They start well, but then struggle to bring their projects to completion. By contrast, Solomon successfully completed his building projects in a little over twenty years.

Establish achievable benchmarks for each month, quarter, and year.

To keep your projects on track until they're done, write your detailed plan with a series of interim goals. Establish achievable benchmarks for each month, quarter, and year. Benchmarks help you to track your progress as you work toward a long-term goal, and they foster a sense of accomplishment as progress is documented.

Then follow through with a consistent effort. Before you know it, your long-term projects will be brought to completion.

A slothful man does not roast his prey, but the precious possession of a man is diligence (Proverbs 12:27).

Is your work always the best it can be?

Scripture: This work is going on with great care and is succeeding in their hands (Ezra 5:8).

Today's Thought: If you want to be successful at work, do your job with great diligence, enthusiasm, and persistence. Pay attention to detail and follow through faithfully.

If you're a manager, establish procedures, systems, and training that will help your employees perform their work efficiently, effectively, and with expertise. Support them with encouragement and constructive feedback that promotes improvement and enhances morale.

> **Do your best work and exercise great care in delivering superior quality, and your customers will be delighted every time.**

Study to learn every important aspect of the products or services you offer, and be able to articulate what constitutes a great product. Just as you expect the products you buy to be free of defects, make sure that you offer only defect-free products to your customers.

Do your best work and exercise great care in delivering superior quality, and your customers will be delighted every time.

He also who is slack in his work is brother to him who destroys (Proverbs 18:9).

Are you working to improve your knowledge and skills?

Scripture: [Ezra] was a scribe skilled in the law of Moses (Ezra 7:6).

Today's Thought: If you want to ensure the success of your business and enhance your own career, make the effort to study and learn all you can about your industry and profession, and take the time to develop the necessary work skills.

Make no excuses for not building your skill and knowledge at work.

If you're new on the job, take good notes during training, ask lots of questions, and apply yourself diligently to mastering your duties. Glean valuable wisdom from experienced coworkers and solicit input about what has helped them in their career development.

Take any available training, enroll in classes that will build your knowledge base, and read business and trade magazines to broaden your perspective.

Make no excuses for not building your skill and knowledge at work. Your preparation and diligence will surely pay off in promotions and increased job satisfaction.

Give her the product of her hands, and let her works praise her in the gates (Proverbs 31:31).

Do you keep good track of inventory in your business?

Scripture: Everything was numbered and weighed, and all the weight was recorded at that time (Ezra 8:34).

Today's Thought: Keeping track of inventory and business assets is important for maintaining profitability. Insist on regular and accurate counts, and don't allow sloppy storage or haphazard inventory control procedures.

Keep track of your inventory and assets, account for every transaction, and watch your profitability grow.

If shortages occur, resolve to find the reason; don't just write off the difference. Spoilage and shrinkage has a way of growing and affecting the bottom line.

Devise and maintain good systems to deter shoplifting. Remember, every dollar lost to theft or inventory shrinkage eats up the profit of ten dollars' worth of sales. Make it clear to your employees that taking stock or supplies home without paying is the same as stealing and won't be tolerated.

Keep track of your inventory and assets, account for every transaction, and watch your profitability grow.

He who tends the fig tree will eat its fruit; and he who cares for his master will be honored (Proverbs 27:18).

Do you insist that your staff accept responsibility for doing their own jobs?

Scripture: Arise! For this matter is your responsibility, but we will be with you; be courageous and act (Ezra 10:4).

Today's Thought: Make it clear to your staff that you expect everyone to take responsibility for their own jobs, and then insist that they produce the desired results.

Helping out in a pinch can build employee morale, but don't make a habit of doing work that should be done by someone else. Bailing out your staff will only increase their dependence on you and reduce everyone's effectiveness.

When employees fall short of the mark, identify what must be accomplished and set a deadline for completion. Do everything in your power to remove roadblocks, but never lose sight of the underlying principle that completing the job is the employee's responsibility.

Offer support and training, and be available to answer questions, but don't let your staff off the hook.

Offer support and training, and be available to answer questions, but don't let your staff off the hook. In order for the entire organization to succeed, everybody must fulfill their primary responsibilities.

Like vinegar to the teeth and smoke to the eyes, so is the lazy one to those who send him (Proverbs 10:26).

When bad news hits your business, do you surrender or keep going?

Scripture: [We are] struck down but not destroyed (2 Corinthians 4:8–9).

Today's Thought: Every company eventually suffers hardship. Whether it's a lost customer, cash-flow worries, production problems, or staff disputes, your business will have its bad days.

The key is how you react. Are you a sad sack and a complainer, or do you maintain a positive, "can do" attitude? To maintain perspective in times of trouble, ask yourself, "What's the worst that can happen as a result of this problem?" Isolated problems are rarely devastating to a business, but when they are repeated or cumulative, the results can be disastrous.

Ask yourself, "What's the worst that can happen as a result of this problem?"

The best response is to take decisive action. First identify what went wrong, then develop a plan to correct the situation for the future.

Don't let the blows of adversity crush you. Be determined to learn from challenging circumstances and improve your business for the long haul.

If you are slack in the day of distress, your strength is limited (Proverbs 24:10).

Do you allow business problems to ruin your entire day?

Scripture: We are afflicted . . . but not crushed (2 Corinthians 4:8).

Today's Thought: Every business leader will face challenges; problems with staff, customer complaints, and difficulties in production are inevitable. At some time in your career, you're bound to feel overwhelmed. The key is in how you respond. Wasting energy by complaining won't help to overcome the situation.

Set other, less important, issues on the back burner, and tackle the important priorities immediately.

When problems threaten to crush you, identify three things that will make a 50 percent difference. Then establish an action plan that involves both you and your staff.

Set other, less important, issues on the back burner, and tackle the important priorities immediately. Improvement will come as you successfully address the biggest issues first. Next, identify lesser issues that you can solve, then keep moving down your list of priorities until everything is back under control.

As you take decisive action, your problems will not crush you, and you will eventually triumph again in your business.

Wisdom is in the presence of the one who has understanding, but the eyes of a fool are on the ends of the earth (Proverbs 17:24).

Topical Index

Steve Marr is the former CEO of the fourth largest import-export firm in America. Currently he consults with ministries and businesses, combining a national and international perspective to create a biblical business model. Steve hosts the radio feature *Business Proverbs,* which is syndicated on nine hundred radio outlets worldwide. His syndicated business column appears in sixteen Christian newspapers from coast to coast, and he has had numerous articles on business and church administration published. For more information, visit www.businessproverbs.com.